The People's Bible Teachings

CHURCH FELLOWSHIP

Working Together for the Truth

John F. Brug

NORTHWESTERN PUBLISHING HOUSE
Milwaukee, Wisconsin

Fourth printing, 1999
Third printing,   1997
Second printing, 1997

Library of Congress Card 96-67792
Northwestern Publishing House
1250 N. 113th St., Milwaukee, WI 53226-3284
© 1996 by Northwestern Publishing House.
Published 1996
Printed in the United States of America
ISBN 0-8100-0595-6

Table of Contents

Editor's Preface

The People's Bible Teachings is a series of books on all of the main doctrinal teachings of the Bible.

Following the pattern set by The People's Bible series, these books are written especially for laypeople. Theological terms, when used, are explained in everyday language so that people can understand them. The authors show how Christian doctrine is drawn directly from clear passages of Scripture and then how those doctrines apply to people's faith and life. Most importantly, these books show how every teaching of Scripture points to Christ, our only Savior.

The authors of The People's Bible Teachings are parish pastors and professors who have had years of experience teaching the Bible. They are men of scholarship and practical insight.

We take this opportunity to express our gratitude to Professor Leroy Dobberstein of Wisconsin Lutheran Seminary, Mequon, Wisconsin, and Professor Thomas Nass of Martin Luther College, New Ulm, Minnesota, for serving as consultants for this series. Their insights and assistance have been invaluable.

We pray that the Lord will use these volumes to help his people grow in their faith, knowledge, and understanding of his saving teachings, which he has revealed to us in the Bible. To God alone be the glory.

Curtis A. Jahn
Series Editor

Introduction

What doctrine would you identify as the special emphasis of the Wisconsin Synod? If a group of Lutherans were asked that question, we hope they would answer, "The doctrine of justification by grace alone through faith alone, especially the truth that God has declared the sins of the whole world forgiven for Christ's sake—that is the special emphasis of the Wisconsin Synod!" Like Paul we say, "We are determined to preach nothing 'except Jesus Christ and him crucified'" (1 Corinthians 2:2). The doctrine of justification by grace alone through faith alone holds first place in our hearts and in our preaching.

Nevertheless, justification is probably not the doctrine that most people would mention as the WELS' trademark. Some might mention our emphasis on the inspiration and inerrancy of Scripture as a conspicuous characteristic that distinguishes the Wisconsin Synod from most Lutheran church bodies in the world today. Because of the great importance of the doctrine of inspiration for preserving all other doctrines of Scripture, we do not object to being closely identified with this doctrine. We would, in fact, be satisfied to have the inerrancy of Scripture listed second among the WELS' doctrinal priorities.

When people list an identifying mark of the Wisconsin Synod, however, the first doctrine that most often comes to their minds is not justification or inspiration, but the doctrine of church fellowship or some aspect of it, such as our practice of closed Communion or our opposition to lodges and scouting. For better or worse, this is the image that many people have of the Wisconsin Synod.

Although we certainly do not place the doctrine of fellowship ahead of justification or inspiration as some people imagine, we should not be embarrassed by people's tendency to associate the name WELS with the doctrine of church fellowship. Our doctrine of church fellowship is drawn from Holy Scripture. Furthermore, it is impossible to retain the other doctrines of Scripture unless we hold on to the scriptural doctrine of fellowship. Failure to practice the biblical principles of church fellowship has been one of the primary causes of the doctrinal deterioration in American and world Lutheranism. We, therefore, need to proclaim this doctrine very boldly.

In recent history the struggle over this doctrine had a great impact in shaping the character of the Wisconsin Synod. The struggle to preserve this doctrine nearly monopolized the attention of WELS synod conventions for more than a decade, spanning the 1950s. The conflict over this doctrine led to widespread disagreement within our synod, to the resignation of the president of our seminary, and to the loss of pastors and congregations, both to the Missouri Synod, which was more liberal in its practice of church fellowship, and to the Church of the Lutheran Confession (CLC), which was perceived as more strict in its practice.

Finally, failure of extended efforts to resolve the disagreement concerning church fellowship led to the end of our working partnership with the Missouri Synod, which had endured for nearly a century, and even to the division of many families. The most traumatic events of this long dispute now lie more than 30 years in the past, but today our position on the doctrine and practice of church fellowship still forms one of the most striking contrasts between the Wisconsin Synod and almost all other

Lutherans. Disagreement about this doctrine also stands as an imposing obstacle in the way of any effort toward reestablishing fellowship with the Missouri Synod, in spite of a recent narrowing of the differences between the two synods in such areas as the doctrine of Scripture.

A careful study of the doctrine of church fellowship is needed today primarily for three reasons:

1. Because the division of the Synodical Conference over the doctrine of church fellowship occurred a generation ago, a review of the decisive events of that struggle is necessary for the new generation, which did not experience this conflict.

2. The pain caused by our separation from the Missouri Synod continues to be felt more than 30 years after the break, especially by families and friends who are divided by it. Some are wondering if the time is drawing near when this breach can be healed.

3. Emotional reactions against our practices concerning church fellowship often arise as a barrier to our outreach efforts and often trouble our own members. The doctrine of church fellowship creates more emotional conflicts than almost any other doctrine in Scripture because it must frequently be applied in the day-to-day life of the church. This doctrine leads us to work with some fellow Christians, but forbids us to work with others. It, therefore, leads to separations in church bodies, in congregations, and in families. This often leads to very emotional encounters and produces intense personal reactions.

For all of these reasons, a thorough knowledge of the doctrine of church fellowship is important for every Christian. In this book we will study this doctrine according to three main divisions: First, we will study the Scripture passages that set forth the biblical principles governing the practice of church fellowship. The doctrine of fellowship that we believe and practice is not a WELS invention, but a doctrine taught by God in Scripture. Second, we will review the historical debate concerning the doctrine of church fellowship that caught WELS in a crossfire between the Missouri Synod from one side and the CLC from the other. Finally, we will consider some applications of this doctrine in the life of the church. Applying this doctrine in a firm but evangelical manner is a way of showing love for our neighbors and giving a clear testimony to the truth.

We now begin our study where every doctrinal discussion must begin—with a study of the pertinent passages of Scripture.

Part I

THE SCRIPTURAL BASIS

OF THE

DOCTRINE OF FELLOWSHIP

1

The Biblical Doctrine of the Church

Before we can study church fellowship, we must review the basic points of the doctrine of the church.

The church is believers

Luther once commented that as a result of the Reformation, every child can now correctly explain the doctrine of the church: The church is the assembly of all people who believe in Christ as their Savior from sin. This is the biblical meaning of the word *church*. Although we sometimes use the word *church* in a loose sense as a name for the building in which we worship or as a name for a congregation or a denomination of Christians, in biblical usage the word *church* always refers to an assembly of people who have faith in Christ, or to the sum total of such believers.

Faith is always the action of an individual. The Holy
Spirit uses the gospel to bring men, women, and children
to faith, one by one. Even on days of mass conversion,
such as Pentecost, each person comes to faith as an individual. All of them must believe for themselves; no one
else can believe for them.

But individual Christians do not remain alone. Everyone who is joined to Christ by faith is also joined to every
other believer. "If we walk in the light, as he is in the
light, we have fellowship with one another, and the blood
of Jesus, his Son, purifies us from all sin" (1 John 1:7).
Through faith in Christ, believers are adopted as members
of the family of God (Galatians 3:26).

The church is one

Just as many bricks are cemented together to form one
building, so many believers are joined together to build
one church of God. "As you come to [Christ], the living
Stone . . . you also, like living stones, are being built into a
spiritual house to be a holy priesthood, offering spiritual
sacrifices acceptable to God through Jesus Christ. You are
a chosen people, a royal priesthood, a holy nation, a people belonging to God, that you may declare the praises of
him who called you out of darkness into his wonderful
light" (1 Peter 2:4,5,9).

Christians are joined together into one body regardless
of their sex, age, wealth, or nationality. Whether they are
male or female; young or old; rich or poor; white or black;
Lutheran, Baptist, or Catholic, all who truly believe in
Jesus as their Savior from sin are members of one family,
the holy Christian church. How wonderful to know that
there is "one Lord, one faith, one baptism; one God and
Father of all" (Ephesians 4:5,6).

Because there is only one way to heaven, namely, faith in Christ, there is only one holy Christian church. All who believe in Jesus Christ as Savior are members of this one church. No unbelievers or hypocrites, however, are members of this church. On judgment day we may find that some people who were lifelong members of a Christian congregation were never members of the holy Christian church because they never had faith. In unusual circumstances believers may have no opportunity to belong to an organized Christian congregation. They are, nevertheless, members of the holy Christian church.

The church is invisible

We call this one true church the *invisible church* because only God knows with certainty who its members are. This is because membership in the church is determined solely by the presence or absence of faith in a person's heart, and only God can read the heart (1 Samuel 16:7). We cannot detect the hypocrites and impostors in the church, but God recognizes every member of his church: "God's solid foundation stands firm, sealed with this inscription: 'The Lord knows those who are his'" (2 Timothy 2:19). On judgment day God will separate the true Christians from the pretenders (Matthew 7:21-23; 25:31-46).

The marks of the church

Although the church is invisible in the sense described above, we can determine where the church is present. Wherever there are believers, the church is present, and there will be believers present wherever the tools that God uses to create saving faith in Christ are being used (Isaiah 55:10,11). Therefore, we can assume that believers are present wherever the truth of the *gospel* is being preached and people are receiving *Baptism* and the *Lord's Supper* as Christ instituted them.

Individual Christians who have been brought to faith by these means of grace will make public confession of the faith that is hidden in their hearts. "It is with your heart that you believe and are justified, and it is with your mouth that you confess and are saved" (Romans 10:10). Wherever we find Christians confessing the faith that has been worked in them by the means of grace, we can assume the presence of true believers, that is, the presence of the church.

Christians seek out one another

Because they are God's children, Christians want to worship God. They want to study God's Word. They want to proclaim the gospel to others. And they want to do these things with other Christians. Whenever Christians meet other believers who confess the same faith they confess, they want to join together with them in worshiping God and sharing the gospel with others. They want to encourage these fellow Christians and to receive admonition and encouragement from them. They want to partake of the Lord's Supper together to receive assurance of forgiveness and to express their unity in Christ. They want to pool their talents and their offerings in joint efforts of Christian education and evangelism. They want to pray for each other. They want to enjoy the company of fellow Christians. For all these reasons Christians join together in congregations.

In doing this they also obey God's commands: "Let the word of Christ dwell in you richly as you teach and admonish one another with all wisdom, and as you sing psalms, hymns and spiritual songs with gratitude in your hearts to

God" (Colossians 3:16) and "Let us consider how we may spur one another on toward love and good deeds. Let us not give up meeting together, as some are in the habit of doing, but let us encourage one another—and all the more as you see the Day approaching" (Hebrews 10:24,25).

Such local congregations of Christians may join together in larger groupings called synods, denominations, or church bodies. Such larger groups of Christians are often the most efficient form of organization for carrying out such assignments of the church as training pastors and teachers, supporting missions, and guarding doctrinal purity.

We call all such organizations of Christians *visible churches* because we can identify the members of such groups by their public acceptance of the confession of that church and by their participation in the activities of that church.

When visible churches teach the Word of God purely, without adding to it or subtracting from it, we call them *orthodox churches*, that is, churches that teach the straight Word of God. When visible churches do not teach the Word of God purely, but mix false teaching with it, we call them *heterodox churches*, that is, churches that teach differently than God's Word teaches. We call even such a false-teaching group a church because of the presence of believers in it. If the gospel, which presents Christ's death as the way to salvation, is still being taught in a heterodox church, there will still be believers there, since the gospel has the power to bring people to faith in spite of the error present alongside it. Nevertheless, the false teaching that is tolerated in a heterodox church is always dangerous to people's faith. Christians have a duty to separate themselves from such error in order to protect themselves from it and to warn others against it.

The biblical doctrine of the church pulls us in two different but complementary directions: we are eager to work together with fellow Christians, but we must avoid working with those who teach and tolerate error.

We are now ready to turn to the main subject of this book: the doctrine and practice of church fellowship.

2

The Definition of Church Fellowship

Fellowship refers to friendly relationships between people and to activities in which they work together to advance their common goals.

Christian fellowship refers first of all to the spiritual relationship that we have with God through faith in Christ. With John we confess, "Our fellowship is with the Father and with his Son, Jesus Christ" (1 John 1:3). Christian fellowship may also refer to the spiritual ties that we have with all believers as members of the invisible church. Each Sunday we confess, "I believe in . . . the holy Christian Church, the communion [that is, the fellowship] of saints" or, "I believe one holy Christian and Apostolic Church."

We cherish this fellowship with God and all believers as a great blessing. We recognize every baptism performed in the name of the Triune God and according to Christ's institution as a valid baptism that makes the recipient a child of God. We do not rebaptize people who come to us from another Christian church. We rejoice when people are brought to saving faith also through the evangelism of churches outside our fellowship. We eagerly look forward to the time when we will enjoy the inheritance of heaven with all believers and all divisions in the church will be healed.

But when we speak about *church fellowship* in this book, we are referring to all activities in which Christians join together as members of visible churches. Church fellowship is every expression of faith in which Christians join together because they are united by their acceptance and confession of all of the teachings of Scripture. We are practicing church fellowship whenever we declare that we are united in doctrine with other Christians and whenever we join with them in activities that express such a shared faith in God's Word.

Since we cannot judge the presence or absence of faith in Christ from a person's heart, we must determine whether we can practice church fellowship with an individual by examining his or her confession of faith. If individuals or groups agree with all of the teachings of Scripture, they should practice church fellowship together. If they disagree in doctrine, they should not practice church fellowship with each other.

It is important, then, to distinguish three aspects of fellowship: (1) the spiritual fellowship that all believers have with God and with each other through faith in Christ, (2) the doctrinal fellowship that is recognized by a shared confession of the truth, and (3) the fellowship that is expressed by joint activities. These three aspects may be summarized by three words: *faith, confession,* and *action.* Faith is worked in us and known with certainty only by God. Judging the existence of this fellowship of faith remains the responsibility of God alone. Although confession and action too are gifts worked in us by God, confession and action can be recognized and carried out by us. We are responsible for judging the confession of all fellow Christians according to Scripture. We are to work together only with those whose confession agrees with all of the truths of Scripture.

We will examine the biblical basis for these claims in Chapters 3 and 4 of this book.

Definition of the unit concept of church fellowship

The biblical concept of church fellowship as taught by the Wisconsin Synod has sometimes been called the *unit concept* of church fellowship. Although this expression never occurs in Scripture, it is an appropriate name, since the Bible teaches that the practice of church fellowship must be treated as a unit in two different respects.

First, when the doctrines of Scripture are being discussed to determine if we can practice fellowship with other Christians, these doctrines must be dealt with as an indivisible unit. Since all the teachings of Scripture have been given by God, we have no right to add anything to them nor to subtract anything from them (Deuteronomy 4:2). Therefore, the practice of church fellowship must be based on agreement in *all* of the doctrines of Scripture. Persistent rejection of even one teaching of Scripture breaks church fellowship between Christians. Some doctrines, such as the doctrines of justification or the means of grace, are more critical for our salvation than others, but we have no right to reject any teaching of Scripture, including its historical statements and its description of creation.

This truth is expressed in the WELS theses on fellowship, which say, "A Christian confession of faith is in principle always a confession to the entire Word of God. The denial, alteration, or suppression of any word of God does not stem from faith but from unbelief" (WELS Theses, B, 2, p. 167 of this book).

Second, the various activities through which we express church fellowship must be dealt with as a unit. Various ways of expressing church fellowship (such as doing mission work together, celebrating the Lord's Supper together, exchanging pastors, transferring members from one congregation to another, and praying together) are merely different ways of expressing the same fellowship of faith. All forms of church fellowship, therefore, require the same level of doctrinal agreement, namely, agreement in all of the doctrines of Scripture. Partial agreement in doctrine does not permit partial practice of fellowship.

We now turn to a study of the Scripture passages that establish these two principles.

3

A Basic Survey of the Scriptural Doctrine

Any attempt to summarize the scriptural basis for the doctrine of church fellowship is faced with an immediate difficulty. The abundance of the biblical material makes it impossible to begin to cover the topic adequately in a short book. At least half of the letters of the New Testament were written primarily to preserve a fellowship that was in jeopardy. Galatians, 1 and 2 Corinthians, and the three letters of John would be prime examples of this category. Several other letters were written to celebrate or strengthen an existing fellowship. Romans and Philippians fall into this category. The pastoral epistles emphasize Paul's directions to young pastors for strengthening and preserving fellowship.

The biblical doctrine of church fellowship is not based only òn a few scattered proof texts, such as Romans 16:17,18, but it is expressed in virtually every letter of the New Testament, as well as in the gospels and the Old Testament. For this reason our study of the scriptural evidence will have to be partial.

John's letters

Two short letters, 2 and 3 John, are the best texts for gaining an overview of the doctrine of church fellowship because they provide a concrete example of the application of the principles of church fellowship to a real-life situation in the New Testament church. John provides us with one of the most beautiful definitions of church fellowship when he states that the goal of his letters is that he and his readers may "work together for the truth" (3 John 8).

This definition of church fellowship is especially important because it shows that church fellowship is first of all a positive concept. Church fellowship is "working together." The primary goal of the doctrine of church fellowship is to lead us to work together with fellow Christians, not to separate from them. In 2 and 3 John the specific form of working together that is under consideration is joint support of missionaries. John and the readers of his letters worked together by sending out missionaries, by recommending these missionaries and their message to others, by offering these men financial support, and by welcoming them as Christian brothers (2 John 10; 3 John 5,6,8,12).

Some have ridiculed the WELS position on church fellowship with statements like "The Wisconsin Synod position on church fellowship is simple. They are against it." Nothing could be further from the truth. We confess with the Scriptures that the practice of church fellowship is first of all something positive: it is "working together." Faith produces in every Christian the desire to join together with other Christians in worship, prayer, and the Lord's Supper. Christians will gladly use their varied gifts to support the teaching and evangelizing mission of the church with their offerings and their time. Christians' energy and concern for church fellowship is focused first of all on finding opportunities to practice fellowship with like-minded Christians. The more we practice a lively, loving fellowship within our congregations and synod, the easier it will be for people to understand the whole doctrine of church fellowship.

When we learned to drive a car, we began by learning how to drive well, but a very necessary next step in driver's training was learning how to avoid crashes. Likewise, when we learn about church fellowship, we begin by learning how to build a strong, loving fellowship with other Christians, but we must also learn how to avoid dangers that will destroy such fellowship.

How can we identify those Christians with whom we may safely practice fellowship? Since we cannot judge the faith in a person's heart, our outward fellowship with another Christian must be based on whether or not that person's *confession* agrees with apostolic doctrine. John says, "We are from God, and whoever knows God listens to us; but whoever is not from God does not listen to us. This is how we recognize the Spirit of truth and the spirit of falsehood" (1 John 4:6). Although church fellowship is defined as working together, not every sort of working together is God-pleasing church fellowship. John defines God-pleasing fellowship as "[working] together *for the truth*" (3 John 8). We, therefore, cannot work together with anyone who departs from the true teachings of Scripture.

John has often been called the apostle of love. This is appropriate, but he could better be called the apostle of truth and love. In these two short letters (2 and 3 John), John mentions *truth* a dozen times. He warns that those who work together with false teachers, either by giving them financial support or by wishing them well, are enemies of the truth. They are guilty of sharing in the false teachers' sin: "Anyone who runs ahead and does not continue in the teaching of Christ does not have God; whoever continues in the teaching has both the Father and the Son. If anyone comes to you and does not bring this teaching, do not take him into your house or welcome him. Anyone who welcomes him shares in his wicked work" (2 John 9-11). Supporters of the truth cannot work together with supporters of falsehood, "for we cannot do anything against the truth, but only for the truth" (2 Corinthians 13:8).

John, therefore, warns against Diotrephes, the leader of the false teachers, by name so that his readers can avoid him (3 John 9,10). Working together for the truth excludes working together with false teachers and their supporters. Of the false teachers John says, "They went out from us, but they did not really belong to us. For if they had belonged to us, they would have remained with us; but their going showed that none of them belonged to us" (1 John 2:19). John urges his readers and us, "Dear friends, do not believe every spirit, but test the spirits to see whether they are from God, because many false prophets have gone out into the world. They are from the world and therefore speak from the viewpoint of the world, and the world listens to them. We are from God, and whoever knows God listens to us; but whoever is not from God does not listen to us. This is how we recognize the Spirit of truth and the spirit of falsehood" (1 John 4:1,5,6). Throughout his letters the apostle of love shows himself to be the apostle of truth as well. We need to follow his example by keeping love and truth together.

The letters in Revelation 2 and 3

In his letters to the seven churches, the apostle John (really Christ speaking through him) shows the same concern for separating truth from falsehood that we have seen in John's earlier letters. These letters to the seven churches beautifully reflect that balance between contending for the truth and acting in love, which Jesus wants to find in his church.

Jesus warns the church at Ephesus that it is losing its first love, but he commends it for testing and identifying false apostles and for refusing to tolerate them (Revelation 2:2,3). Jesus rebukes the churches at Pergamum and Thyatira for tolerating false teachers who encourage people to ignore God's law (Revelation 2:14-16,20,21).

Today some people claim that the church needs more love and less zeal for doctrinal truth, but neither truth nor love can serve its purpose unless both are kept together. If we really want to help our neighbor, but in ignorance we are telling him falsehoods that will lead him to hell, such "love" is really a deadly device of Satan. If we know the truth, but we proclaim it in an arrogant, self-righteous way, we place a stumbling block in the way of our neighbor. "Love" without knowledge of the truth is misguided zeal that leads souls away from God (Romans 10:1-3). On the other hand, if we know the truth, but we do not have enough love to share it with others, the truth cannot accomplish its purpose. If we know God's law, but we refuse to correct a neighbor who is caught in error, this is not love but sinful selfishness. If we know the gospel, but we withhold it from those crushed by the burden of sin, the gospel cannot accomplish its healing purpose.

We must share the truth in a gentle, tactful way, but to withhold the truth from someone is never love. If one night you saw that your neighbors' house was on fire, but you failed to scream warnings to them because you did not want to disturb their sleep, everyone would call you stupid and uncaring. But when false teaching is placing people's souls in danger of the eternal fires of hell, we are urged to keep quiet about it and to call such silence love. What is more unloving—to fail to warn people against a fire that can destroy their bodies or to fail to warn them against a false doctrine that can destroy their souls? Failure to warn of danger is never love.

In the Bible *love* does not refer to a warm feeling about somebody. Love is not liking someone for the way that person happens to be but, rather, doing whatever is necessary to help him or her, even at great cost to ourselves. "God demonstrates his own love for us in this: While we were still sinners, Christ died for us" (Romans 5:8). "This is how we know what love is: Jesus Christ laid down his life for us" (1 John 3:16). We love our neighbors not by having a warm fuzzy feeling about them, but by declaring to them the whole Word of God. "This is how we know that we love the children of God: by loving God and carrying out his commands" (1 John 5:2).

The church needs to keep truth and love in balance just as much as an airplane needs two wings to fly. If either wing is lost, the plane will crash. If either truth or love is lost, the church cannot carry out its mission. Truth and love are not opposites. They are not rivals. They are partners that dare not be separated.

When we are told that we must choose between truth and love, we must remember God's definition of love. Real love is, above all else, that we love all of God's truth: "If you love me, you will obey what I command. And I will ask the Father, and he will give you another Counselor to be with you forever—the Spirit of truth. The world cannot accept him, because it neither sees him nor knows him. But you know him, for he lives with you and will be in you" (John 14:15-17).

We must ask frankly whether the reluctance of people today to speak against false teaching is due to greater love for other people or to less love for God's Word. If we love God's truth, we will share all of it with our neighbors, especially when they are in danger of being led astray by false teachers. Telling the truth is the highest expression of love.

Paul urged young pastor Timothy, "Stay there in Ephesus so that you may command certain men not to teach false doctrines any longer. The goal of this command is love, which comes from a pure heart and a good conscience and a sincere faith" (1 Timothy 1:3,5). The greatest love we can show for people is to guard them against the soul-destroying poison of false doctrine by telling them the truth.

Paul's pastoral letters

Paul's concern for true doctrine shows itself throughout his three pastoral letters to Timothy and Titus. He piles one admonition on another as he urges Timothy to oppose false teachers (1 Timothy 1:3-5). Like John, Paul identifies such false teachers by name so that people can be on the lookout against them (1 Timothy 1:20; 2 Timothy 2:17,18; 4:14). Paul delivers a strong warning against false teachers who will come, bringing doctrines of the devil, such as forbidding marriage and prohibiting certain foods. It is the duty of a good minister to warn against such teachings and the teachers who bring them (1 Timothy 4:1-6).

Paul warns that, in spite of the efforts of faithful teachers, false teachers will flourish in the last days. They will be popular because they will tell people what they want to hear, even condoning people's immoral lifestyles (2 Timothy 3:1-9; 4:3,4).

Anyone who teaches differently than the sound words of the Lord Jesus Christ is conceited and knows nothing (1 Timothy 6:3,4). If such false teachers reject the warnings against their teaching, they themselves are to be rejected by those who love God's truth: "Warn a divisive person once, and then warn him a second time. After that, have nothing to do with him" (Titus 3:10).

A faithful minister is to guard both his life and his doctrine so that he may save himself and others (1 Timothy 4:16). To prepare himself to battle such false teachers, God's servant must carefully study the Holy Scriptures so that he can separate truth from error. "Do your best to present yourself to God as one approved, a workman who does not need to be ashamed and who correctly handles the word of truth" (2 Timothy 2:15). "Evil men and impostors will go from bad to worse, deceiving and being deceived. But as for you, continue in what you have learned and have become convinced of, because you know those from whom you learned it, and how from infancy you have known the holy Scriptures, which are able to make you wise for salvation through faith in Christ Jesus. All Scripture is God-breathed and is useful for teaching, rebuking, correcting and training in righteousness, so that the man of God may be thoroughly equipped for every good work" (2 Timothy 3:13-17).

Although God's workmen are to oppose falsehood, they are to avoid disputes that are mere word-battles. Because their primary aim is not to win arguments but to win people, they are to gently instruct those who have fallen into error, in hopes of regaining them for the truth (2 Timothy 2:14-26).

Christians are to be careful about whom they put into positions of leadership in the church, lest they become guilty of sponsoring the sins of others (1 Timothy 5:22).

Conclusion

This survey of the letters of John and the pastoral letters of Paul has shown that a concern for doctrinal unity as the basis for the practice of church fellowship is not an incidental matter for the writers of the New Testament, but runs through all their work. The space limitations of this book do not permit us to survey this doctrine throughout all the books of the Bible in the same detail. Therefore, we must limit ourselves to the study of representative passages from other New Testament books. We will focus on passages that address the two questions that are the main disputed issues in connection with this doctrine: (1) Does Scripture require agreement in *all* doctrines as a basis for the practice of church fellowship? (2) Do some expressions of fellowship, such as joint prayer or cooperation in charitable work, require a lesser degree of doctrinal agreement than sharing the Lord's Supper or exchanging pulpits?

4

Agreement in All Doctrines
Is Necessary for Fellowship

Unity in doctrine not limited to only certain doctrines

Nothing in Scripture suggests that the unity of faith that is required for the outward expression of church fellowship is limited to agreement only in the doctrine of justification or a few fundamental doctrines. It is true that many of the doctrinal disputes referred to in the New Testament involved fundamental doctrines. When Paul wrote to the Galatians, he was battling a denial of the doctrine of justification by grace alone, through faith alone. In his epistles John appears to be battling a heresy that denied Jesus' humanity.

At the same time, the New Testament cites many other types of doctrinal error as divisive of fellowship, including denying the resurrection of the body (2 Timothy 2:18), teaching Christians that they could disregard God's commandments since the forgiveness of sins was free (Revelation 2, 3; Jude 3-10; 2 Peter 2:1-3,13-20), forbidding marriage and prohibiting certain foods (1 Timothy 4:3), and quarreling about genealogies and the law (Titus 3:9). This list is comprehensive enough to demonstrate that the apostles' concern for doctrinal purity was not limited to a few key doctrines.

The Bible closes with the solemn warning that a curse rests on anyone who adds *anything* to the Bible or who subtracts *anything* from it: "I warn everyone who hears the words of the prophecy of this book: If anyone adds anything to them, God will add to him the plagues described in this book. And if anyone takes words away from this book of prophecy, God will take away from him his share in the tree of life and in the holy city, which are described in this book" (Revelation 22:18,19). Since no one has the right to add to or subtract anything from the Bible, we cannot work together with those who reject any teachings of the Bible.

It is true that, just as some doses of poison are more deadly than others, the loss of certain doctrines, such as the doctrines of justification or the deity of Christ, is more deadly to faith than the loss of other doctrines, such as a correct understanding of the doctrine of the Antichrist. But just as we want no poison in our food, not even the unintentional inclusion of small amounts of cancer-causing substances, so we can tolerate no poison in our spiritual food, that is, the teachings of Scripture that feed our faith. We must separate ourselves from everyone who clings to false teaching in spite of warnings and admonition.

Adiaphora not divisive of fellowship

Agreement in adiaphora (things that God has neither commanded nor forbidden) and ceremonies is not necessary for fellowship. In Romans 14 Paul says:

> Accept him whose faith is weak, without passing judgment on disputable matters. The man who eats everything must not look down on him who does not, and the man who does not eat everything must not condemn the man who does, for God has accepted him. One man considers one day more sacred than another; another man considers every day alike. Each one should be fully convinced in his own mind. He who regards one day as special, does so to the Lord. He who eats meat, eats to the Lord, for he gives thanks to God; and he who abstains, does so to the Lord and gives thanks to God. Therefore let us stop passing judgment on one another. Instead, make up your mind not to put any stumbling block or obstacle in your brother's way. Let us therefore make every effort to do what leads to peace and to mutual edification (verses 1,3,5,6,13,19).

On another occasion Paul said, "Therefore do not let anyone judge you by what you eat or drink, or with regard to a religious festival, a New Moon celebration or a Sabbath day" (Colossians 2:16).

Christians do not have to use the same liturgy or enjoy the same style of worship to be in fellowship with each other. Worship styles in our world mission fields are often quite different than those in an American suburban WELS congregation. Some Christians may baptize by immersion; some may baptize by pouring water on the baby. Christians are not required to have the same system of church government or all of the same forms of ministry. We have a ministry of Lutheran elementary school teachers. Many denominations do not. Christians do not have to follow the same diet or wear the same styles in order to practice fellowship together. Some Christians may choose to abstain from alcoholic beverages; others may use them in moderation. Such differences of opinion and practice are not divisive of church fellowship unless one party insists that its way is the only right way (Galatians 5:1). There is room for much diversity of *custom* in the church, but nothing in the New Testament offers any basis for excluding any *doctrine* from the unity needed for fellowship.

Our Lutheran Confessions state this principle in Article VII of the Augsburg Confession: "For the true unity of the church it is enough to agree concerning the teaching of the Gospel and the administration of the sacraments. It is not necessary that human traditions or rites and ceremonies, instituted by men, should be alike everywhere."[1] When the Augsburg Confession speaks here of "the teaching of the Gospel," it is not making a distinction between one teaching of Scripture as opposed to other scriptural teachings. The distinction is between the doctrine of the gospel and human traditions and ceremonies. "The teaching of the Gospel" is used here in a broad sense and refers to every teaching our Lord has revealed to us in Scripture.

Unity in doctrine does not require uniformity in terminology

Complete uniformity in the use of doctrinal terminology is not necessary for church fellowship. We should not battle about mere words (2 Timothy 2:14-26). In 2 Thessalonians 2:3, Paul warns against a false teacher called the "man of sin" (KJV) or the "man of lawlessness" (NIV). In 1 John 4:3, John calls this same false teacher the "Antichrist." Even though they used different names for this false teacher, Paul and John agreed on the doctrine concerning his coming. It, therefore, would not be right to deny fellowship to someone who had the same teaching that we have, but who used different words to express it. It is, however, desirable to agree on common terminology within a church body to avoid confusing people who are receiving instruction.

Difference of words does not necessarily mean difference of doctrine, but we also need to be alert for the opposite danger. Use of the same words may be intended to hide differences of doctrine. False teachers often try to disguise their false teaching by twisting the meaning of the words that the orthodox church uses to express its teaching. For example, when false teachers call the Bible infallible, they mean that it never fails to accomplish God's purpose even though it contains many errors. Such a use of *infallible* is intended to fool orthodox Christians, who use the word to assert that the Bible is entirely without error. Such deception may mislead faithful Christians into thinking that false teachers are proclaimers of the truth who deserve their help and support.

For this reason, the church has sometimes found it necessary to insist on specific, unambiguous terminology to "smoke out" false teachers. The need for such clear terminology is one reason that the church has composed creeds and confessions. The false teachers' refusal to accept these creeds exposes their deception and warns people to avoid them.

We should briefly mention that it would also be wrong to divide the church on the basis of loyalty to a particular person (1 Corinthians 1:11-13; 3:21-23) or to refuse fellowship to anyone on the basis of race, sex, or economic status (Galatians 3:28; James 2:1-5).

Scripture makes no exceptions on doctrines

Although agreement in adiaphora, ceremonies, and wording is not necessary for fellowship, complete agreement in doctrine is necessary. The New Testament admonitions to doctrinal unity and its warnings against false doctrine are all-inclusive, general statements that in no way imply there are some scriptural doctrines that can safely be omitted or that there are some false teachings that can safely be tolerated:

> [Teach] them to obey *everything* I have commanded you (Matthew 28:20).

> Make every effort to keep the unity of the Spirit through the bond of peace. It was [Christ] who gave some to be apostles, some to be prophets, some to be evangelists, and some to be pastors and teachers, to prepare God's people for works of service, so that the body of Christ may be built up until we all reach *unity in the faith* and in the knowledge of the Son of God and become mature, attaining to *the whole measure of the fullness of Christ.* Then we will no longer be infants, tossed back and forth by the waves, and blown here and there by every wind of teaching and by the cunning and craftiness of men in their deceitful scheming. Instead, speaking the truth in love, we will in *all things* grow up into him who is the Head, that is, Christ (Ephesians 4:3,11-15).

> I have not hesitated to proclaim to you *the whole will of God.* Keep watch over yourselves and all the flock of which the Holy Spirit has made you overseers. Be shepherds of the church of God, which he bought with his own blood. I know that after I leave, savage wolves will come in among you and will not spare the flock. Even from your own number men will arise and distort the truth in order to draw away disciples after them. So be on your guard! (Acts 20:27-31).

I appeal to you, brothers, in the name of our Lord Jesus Christ, that all of you agree with one another so that there may be no divisions among you and that you may *be perfectly united in mind and thought* (1 Corinthians 1:10).

If anyone takes words away from this book of prophecy, God will take away from him his share in the tree of life (Revelation 22:19).

Command certain men not to teach false doctrines any longer nor to devote themselves to myths and endless genealogies (1 Timothy 1:3,4).

If anyone teaches false doctrines and does not agree to the sound instruction of our Lord Jesus Christ and to godly teaching, he is conceited and understands nothing (1 Timothy 6:3,4).

If you hold to my teaching, you are really my disciples (John 8:31).

If anyone speaks, he should do it as one speaking the very words of God (1 Peter 4:11).

May the God who gives endurance and encouragement give you a spirit of unity among yourselves as you follow Christ Jesus, so that with one heart and mouth you may glorify the God and Father of our Lord Jesus Christ (Romans 15:5,6).

None of these passages nor any of the many other similar passages in the New Testament offers even a hint of support for the idea that any doctrine of Scripture can be dispensed with or that any doctrinal error can be accepted as harmless. In Article X of the Formula of Concord, our Lutheran Confessions state, "We believe, teach, and confess that no church should condemn another because it has fewer or more external ceremonies not commanded by

God, as long as there is mutual agreement *in doctrine and in all its articles.*"[2]

Romans 16:17,18

Since Romans 16:17,18 is undoubtedly the passage most often quoted on this topic, we will single it out for special attention: "I urge you, brothers, to watch out for those who cause divisions and put obstacles in your way that are contrary to the teaching you have learned. Keep away from them. For such people are not serving our Lord Christ, but their own appetites. By smooth talk and flattery they deceive the minds of naive people."

This passage follows immediately after a long expression of church fellowship, the Christian greetings and commendations that Paul extends in Romans 16:1-16. In contrast to the command "greet," which dominates verses 1-16, Paul introduces a very different command in verse 17—"keep away." Both commands are addressed to the same people, to Paul's brothers and sisters in the faith, the members of the congregation at Rome. The two commands, however, govern their relationship with two different groups of people.

The Roman Christians were in spiritual fellowship with Paul because they were united with him by their faith in Christ. They were also in church fellowship with Paul since they accepted all of the doctrine that Paul had taught throughout his letter and that he taught in all his mission fields. For this reason Paul is confident that they will want to be taught by him when he passes through Rome and that they will want to support his new mission project in Spain (Romans 15:23,24). He, therefore, urges them to greet all those at Rome who share their common faith. But in verse 17 he warns them to keep away from all those who do not share that faith.

He says they should "watch out" for them. Because false teachers disguise themselves, the Roman Christians must continually be on the lookout so that they will not be deceived by the smooth talk of false teachers.

Who are the people the Romans are to keep away from? They are described as people who "are causing divisions and setting up traps which cause people to fall into sin, contrary to the teaching you have learned" (literal translation). The Greek verb rendered "are causing divisions" describes an action that is continuous and habitual. The people to be avoided are not teachers who inadvertently misspeak. They are not naive or uninformed victims who unknowingly follow false doctrine. They are teachers who persist in their false doctrine and their sinful conduct in spite of warnings against it. They are serving "their own appetites"; that is, they are not serving Christ, but their own egos, desires, lusts, intellect, and reason. They may look like servants of Christ to the casual observer, but no one ever serves Christ by any false teaching. Since their man-made teachings appeal to human reason and to sinful desires, the false teachers find willing followers who join in their sin. Both the teachers and their supporters are to be avoided.

There is no indication in the text that Paul is limiting his condemnation to specific false teachers who were present in Rome. He is stating a general principle that has a universal application. When Christians recognize false teachers who continue in their error in spite of admonition, they are to keep away from them; that is, they are to make a clean break from them. "Divisions and . . . traps which cause people to fall into sin" is a phrase broad enough to apply to any false teaching, whether it involves doctrine or morality. "The teaching you have learned" is a comprehensive phrase that includes everything the Roman Christians had been taught by the apostles and their assistants.

It should be noted in passing that Paul labels the false teachers as people "who cause divisions" in the church. It has always been the style of false teachers to blame the divisions in the church on the true teachers who oppose their false teaching and separate from them. The ungodly king Ahab labeled the prophet Elijah as the "troubler of Israel" (1 Kings 18:17). But Elijah's denunciation of the wicked idolatry of Ahab and Jezebel was not the cause of the division in Israel. Ahab and Jezebel had divided Israel by installing the worship of Baal alongside the worship of the Lord as it had been taught by Moses (verse 18). Ahab and Jezebel were the real troublers of Israel.

Luther did not divide the church by steadfastly opposing the false teachings of the pope at Rome. The pope and his adherents had divided the church by introducing new doctrines contrary to the doctrines the apostles had taught. Luther was trying to reunite the church on the basis of a return to apostolic doctrine. False teachers always try to blame the divisions in the church on the true teachers who oppose them and who separate from them, but Scripture places the blame for division in the church where it belongs—on the false teachers who depart from the unity produced by obedience to God's Word.

Matthew 7

We have seen that Scripture commands us to judge the doctrine of all teachers of religion so that we may avoid those whose teaching departs from God's Word. It also warns us not to do this in a harsh or self-righteous spirit.

Jesus brings both of these concerns together in the conclusion of the Sermon on the Mount:

> Watch out for false prophets. They come to you in sheep's
> clothing, but inwardly they are ferocious wolves. By their
> fruit you will recognize them. . . . Not everyone who says
> to me, "Lord, Lord," will enter the kingdom of heaven, but
> only he who does the will of my Father who is in heaven.
> Many will say to me on that day, "Lord, Lord, did we not
> prophesy in your name, and in your name drive out
> demons and perform many miracles?" Then I will tell
> them plainly, "I never knew you. Away from me, you evil-
> doers!"(Matthew 7:15,16,21-23).

False teachers are hard to detect since they disguise
themselves as true teachers (2 Corinthians 11:13-15).
Therefore, we must study carefully all of God's Word so
that we can judge every teacher of religion, as well as
every teaching that comes our way, so that we will be able
to avoid that which is contrary to God's Word. The Bere-
ans, who checked Paul's teaching by going to the Scriptures, are a model of such Bible study (Acts 17:11). We
must judge every teacher by the fruit he produces, that is,
by his teaching.

But in the same chapter in which Jesus commands us to
judge teachers, he warns us against self-righteous judging
of either the lives or beliefs of others:

> Do not judge, or you too will be judged. For in the same
> way you judge others, you will be judged, and with the
> measure you use, it will be measured to you. Why do you
> look at the speck of sawdust in your brother's eye and pay
> no attention to the plank in your own eye? How can you
> say to your brother, "Let me take the speck out of your
> eye," when all the time there is a plank in your own eye?
> You hypocrite, first take the plank out of your own eye,

and then you will see clearly to remove the speck from
your brother's eye (Matthew 7:1-5).

We must first be judged by God's Word so that we recognize our own sins and errors. Then we will see clearly to
warn others against their sin.

Immediately following this command not to judge self-
righteously, Jesus uses shocking language as he commands
us to separate ourselves from those who cling to error: "Do
not give dogs what is sacred; do not throw your pearls to
pigs. If you do, they may trample them under their feet,
and then turn and tear you to pieces" (Matthew 7:6). We
cannot share the means of grace with those who despise
God and his Word. We cannot practice fellowship with
those who support error or live in immorality. Scripture
commands us to make strong judgments, but it warns us to
make them with humility and patient love.

When we separate from false teachers, we are not judging the faith of their hearts, which no human can judge.
That judgment we leave to Christ (Matthew 7:23). But we
are to judge their teaching and their conduct, which can
be judged on the basis of Scripture. From such false teaching and from those who cling to it, we must separate ourselves as Jesus commands (Matthew 7:15).

Jesus' strong opposition to false teachers within the
church is not limited to Matthew 7, but is found throughout the gospels (Matthew 15:1-14; 16:5-12; 23:1-36;
24:4-14). When the apostles issued strong warnings to
avoid false teachers, they were simply following in their
Master's footsteps.

5

All Ways of Expressing Fellowship Are a Unit

Nothing in Scripture suggests that some ways of practicing church fellowship require less agreement in doctrine than others. In the New Testament all expressions of fellowship are treated as a unit. They are all ways of expressing the same oneness of faith.

Various ways of expressing fellowship

Christians express fellowship with one another when they encourage each other by worshiping together (Hebrews 10:24,25; Colossians 3:16). Quite clearly, sharing the Lord's Supper is an expression of fellowship between the participants: "Is not the cup of thanksgiving for which we give thanks a participation in the blood of Christ? And is not the bread that we break a participation in the body of Christ? Because there is one loaf, *we, who are many, are one body, for we all partake of the one loaf*" (1 Corinthians 10:16,17). We, therefore, must worship and commune only with Christians with whom we are in doctrinal agreement. We must not invite pastors who do not agree with our doctrine to preach in our churches, nor must our pastors preach in theirs. We must not attend Communion with people who reject any of the teachings of the Bible.

Anyone who provides financial support to a teacher of religion is expressing fellowship with him. This is true whether the teacher is one's own pastor or someone whose work is being done far away. Christians who support a pastor have not entered a business transaction with him, but a mutual sharing of material and spiritual blessings. "Anyone who receives instruction in the word must share all good things with his instructor" (Galatians 6:6). The pastor shares with his congregation the spiritual treasures he has received through his training in the Word. The members in turn share their material treasures with the pastor. Paul says, "If we have sown spiritual seed among you, is it too much if we reap a material harvest from you? . . . The Lord has commanded that those who preach the gospel should receive their living from the gospel" (1 Corinthians 9:11,14).

The Philippians had become partners in Paul's work through the financial support they sent him (Philippians 1:5; 4:15). On the other hand, those who support or encourage false teachers are partners in their evil deeds. "If anyone comes to you and does not bring this teaching, do not take him into your house or welcome him. Anyone who welcomes him shares in his wicked work" (2 John 10,11). Those who support false teachers are accomplices of an evil act just as much as the individual who drives the getaway car for a bank robber or the person who hides a fleeing murderer. Anyone who gives money to a false teacher is certainly not obeying Scripture's command to separate from him.

Fellowship may also be expressed by brotherly consultations to resolve doctrinal questions, by joint doctrinal resolutions, by mutual recognition of each other's ministries, and by agreement to divide mission fields (Acts 15:1-32; Galatians 2:1-10). We, therefore, do not participate in doctrinal studies with heterodox churches (except in efforts to eliminate the errors that separate them from us), nor do we cooperate with them in producing instructional materials, nor do we agree to divide responsibility for mission fields with them.

Church fellowship may be expressed by a handshake (Galatians 2:9); by a kiss (Romans 16:16); or by the exchange of fraternal greetings, which is so common in Paul's letters (Romans 16:1-16). Fellowship is also expressed by the "letters of recommendation" that are common in the New Testament (Romans 16:1-3; 2 Corinthians 8:16-23; 3 John 12). Present-day practices that are parallel to these biblical customs include the handshake given at an ordination, a confirmation, or a colloquy; the exchange of congratulations and greetings offered at church anniversaries and conventions; and letters of transfer. We, therefore, do not transfer members to heterodox churches, nor do we send heterodox churches congratulations and best wishes for their work.

"Cooperation in externals"

Today cooperation in Christian charity work is sometimes regarded as mere "cooperation in externals," but it was not so regarded in the New Testament. The Macedonians urgently pleaded with Paul for the privilege of sharing in (that is, having fellowship in) the charitable service to the saints in Jerusalem (2 Corinthians 8:4). The goal of this charitable work was not merely to relieve human need, but to join together in glorifying God. "This service that you perform is not only supplying the needs of God's people but is also overflowing in many expressions of thanks to God. Because of the service by which you have proved yourselves, men will praise God for the obedience that accompanies your confession of the gospel of Christ" (2 Corinthians 9:12,13). The spiritual motivation and the fellowship that are an essential part of Christian charity are emphasized throughout 2 Corinthians 8 and 9.

Prayer fellowship

There are times when praying *for* a person is an expression of fellowship with him, for example, when we pray for the success of his ministry (Romans 15:30-32; 2 Corinthians 1:11). There are, of course, other circumstances when praying for a person is not an expression of fellowship, as when Christians pray for the enemies of the church. Praying *with* a person, however, is always an expression of fellowship.

The dispute concerning the doctrine of prayer fellowship in American Lutheranism centered on the question "May we pray together with people who are not in doctrinal agreement with us?"

The New Testament does not treat prayer fellowship separately from other forms of fellowship. Prayer as an expression of fellowship is simply treated as one element among many others. The early Christians "devoted themselves to the apostles' teaching and to the fellowship, to the breaking of bread and to prayer" (Acts 2:42). *There is, therefore, nothing in Scripture to suggest that prayer should be treated any differently from any other expression of fellowship.* Since God-pleasing prayer always flows from faith, every prayer is either an expression of faith (and therefore an act of worship), or it is an abomination. There is no middle ground. If true prayer is always an act of worship, joint prayer calls for the same unity of doctrine as any other act of worship.

In some ways the issue of joint prayer is similar to the issue of infant baptism. The Bible does not specifically say "baptize babies," but the unrestricted command "baptize all nations" includes children unless valid scriptural reasons can be cited for excluding them. In the same way, the unrestricted commands to "keep away" from false teachers (Romans 16:17) and to "have nothing to do with [them]" (Titus 3:10) certainly prohibit all expressions of fellowship with them, including prayer. "Have nothing to do with [them]" and "keep away from them" cannot mean "pray with them." The issue of prayer fellowship will be discussed in more detail in the historical and practical sections of this book.

No "levels of fellowship" in Scripture

There is no scriptural basis for dividing the various expressions of fellowship into different levels that require different degrees of doctrinal agreement. Different forms of fellowship are simply different ways of expressing one and the same unity of faith. The only distinction between them is that some of these acts, such as any use of the means of grace and prayer, are by their very nature always expressions of faith, but other acts, such as a handshake, a kiss, or giving to charity, may also be done in a secular context and are, therefore, not always expressions of religious fellowship. It depends on the context in which they are done.

Conclusion

On the basis of the Scripture passages we have studied, it is our conviction that all outward expressions of church fellowship should be practiced only among those who agree in *all* doctrines of Scripture. Since this principle applies to church bodies, to congregations, and to individuals, it sometimes has been called the principle of *confessional fellowship* in order to make it clear that its application is not limited to formal relationships between church bodies. However, in this book the term *church fellowship*, which is more familiar to us, has been retained to describe all relationships between Christians on any level, since all are relationships between members of the church.

It is also our conviction that agreement in all the doctrines of Scripture forms the necessary prerequisite for the joint practice of *all expressions* of church fellowship, whether altar and pulpit fellowship, joint prayer, or any other expression of fellowship. Unfortunately, this belief has not been shared by the majority of American Lutherans, as we shall see in Part II of this book.

6

Preserving and Extending Fellowship

There are few joys greater than Christian fellowship. "How good and pleasant it is when brothers live together in unity! It is like precious oil poured on the head, running down on the beard, running down on Aaron's beard, down upon the collar of his robes. It is as if the dew of Hermon were falling on Mount Zion. For there the LORD bestows his blessing, even life forevermore" (Psalm 133). Christian fellowship is a blessing to celebrate and to cherish.

Working to preserve and strengthen fellowship

Working together with those who hold to the truth and turning away from those who persist in error does not exhaust our responsibility for this blessed fellowship. We must also work hard to preserve this fellowship whenever it is threatened by the intrusion of sin and error. "Make every effort to keep the unity of the Spirit through the bond of peace" (Ephesians 4:3).

We strengthen existing ties of fellowship when our words and deeds display that love for fellow Christians that we feel in our hearts. "Now that you have purified yourselves by obeying the truth so that you have sincere love for your brothers, love one another deeply, from the heart" (1 Peter 1:22).

One way of showing this love is by helping our fellow Christians with their bodily needs. "Therefore, as we have opportunity, let us do good to all people, especially to those who belong to the family of believers" (Galatians 6:10). "If anyone has material possessions and sees his brother in need but has no pity on him, how can the love of God be in him? Dear children, let us not love with words or tongue but with actions and in truth. This then is how we know that we belong to the truth, and how we set our hearts at rest in his presence" (1 John 3:17-19). We strive to live so that Jesus' description will be true of us: "By this all men will know that you are my disciples, if you love one another" (John 13:35).

We strengthen our ties with fellow believers when we build up the church's defenses against error. It is the duty of our pastors and teachers to carefully instruct all the members of the congregation in all the truths of God's Word so that they are strengthened in their ability to detect and oppose false teaching:

> [Christ] gave some to be apostles, some to be prophets, some to be evangelists, and some to be pastors and teach-ers, to prepare God's people for works of service, so that the body of Christ may be built up until we all reach unity

in the faith and in the knowledge of the Son of God and become mature, attaining to the whole measure of the fullness of Christ. Then we will no longer be infants, tossed back and forth by the waves, and blown here and there by every wind of teaching and by the cunning and craftiness of men in their deceitful scheming. Instead, speaking the truth in love, we will in all things grow up into him who is the Head, that is, Christ. From him the whole body, joined and held together by every supporting ligament, grows and builds itself up in love, as each part does its work (Ephesians 4:11-16).

We strengthen the unity of the church by respecting and supporting faithful teachers of the Word. Paul commanded, "Therefore encourage one another and build each other up, just as in fact you are doing. Now we ask you, brothers, to respect those who work hard among you, who are over you in the Lord and who admonish you. Hold them in the highest regard in love because of their work. Live in peace with each other" (1 Thessalonians 5:11-13). "The elders who direct the affairs of the church well are worthy of double honor, especially those whose work is preaching and teaching" (1 Timothy 5:17). John said,

I have no greater joy than to hear that my children are walking in the truth. Dear friend, you are faithful in what you are doing for the brothers, even though they are strangers to you. They have told the church about your love. You will do well to send them on their way in a manner worthy of God. It was for the sake of the Name that they went out, receiving no help from the pagans. We ought therefore to show hospitality to such men so that we may work together for the truth (3 John 4-8).

We preserve fellowship by gently warning a brother or sister who has fallen into error. "The Lord's servant must not quarrel; instead, he must be kind to everyone, able to teach, not resentful. Those who oppose him he must gently instruct, in the hope that God will grant them repentance leading them to a knowledge of the truth, and that they will come to their senses and escape from the trap of the devil, who has taken them captive to do his will" (2 Timothy 2:24-26).

Weak brothers versus persistent errorists

When we deliver warnings against false teaching, we distinguish weak brothers and sisters who have been victimized by false teachers from the persistent promoters of false doctrine: "'In the last times there will be *scoffers* who will follow their own ungodly desires.' These are the men who divide you, who follow mere natural instincts and do not have the Spirit. Be merciful to *those who doubt*; snatch others from the fire and save them; to others show mercy, mixed with fear—hating even the clothing stained by corrupted flesh" (Jude 18,19,22,23). Jesus reserved his harshest tone for the false teachers; he sympathized with their victims (Matthew 23). Paul spoke more harshly of the false teachers than of their victims in Galatia and Corinth. Nevertheless, if those who have been taken in by the false teachers continue to support them even after they have been warned against them, we can no longer consider them to be weak brothers and sisters. We must recognize them as supporters of error and avoid them.

We remember how patiently Jesus dealt with the weakness of his disciples as he instructed them. Our WELS theses on fellowship emphasize our responsibility to the weak: "Weakness of faith is in itself not a reason for terminating church fellowship, but rather an inducement for practicing it vigorously to help one another in overcoming our individual weaknesses. In precept and example, Scripture abounds with exhortations to pay our full debt of love toward the weak" (WELS Theses, B, 4, p. 168 of this book).

We turn away from the adherents of false teaching only after they have rejected our admonition: "Warn a divisive person once, and then warn him a second time. After that, have nothing to do with him" (Titus 3:10). The same principle also applies when a fellow believer is persisting in a sin. "If your brother sins against you, go and show him his fault, just between the two of you. If he listens to you, you have won your brother over. But if he will not listen, take one or two others along, so that 'every matter may be established by the testimony of two or three witnesses.' If he refuses to listen to them, tell it to the church; and if he refuses to listen even to the church, treat him as you would a pagan or a tax collector" (Matthew 18:15-17).

On the basis of these passages, our WELS theses say, "Persistent adherence to false doctrine and practice calls for termination of church fellowship." Persistent errorists are those "who in spite of patient admonition persistently adhere to an error in doctrine or practice, demand recognition for their error, and make propaganda for it" (WELS Theses, B, 5 and 5b, p. 169 of this book).

Doctrinal discipline at the congregational level

We exercise these principles on a congregational level when the voters assembly practices excommunication and termination of fellowship. We use the term *excommunication* for the removal of an individual who, in spite of brotherly admonition, refuses to repent of a sin, denies a doctrine that is essential to salvation, or knowingly rejects any teaching of Scripture (WELS Theses, B, 5a, p. 169 of this book). When the congregation excommunicates such a person, it has reached the conclusion that the person's manifest impenitence demonstrates that he or she is an unbeliever who has lost faith and forgiveness.

We commonly use a term like *termination of fellowship* when a congregation must exclude a member because he or she clings to an error in doctrine or practice that does not destroy the foundation of saving faith, and the error-ist, in spite of warning, remains convinced that his or her error is, in fact, the teaching of Scripture (WELS Theses B, 5b, p. 169,170 of this book). When the voters assembly excludes such a person from the congregation, it has not concluded that the person has lost saving faith, but that the individual is persistently holding to a false doctrine that makes it impossible to remain in fellowship with him. Such an error is a sin that places faith in jeopardy, but it may be a matter of ignorance and error that has not destroyed saving faith.

It is also the responsibility of the church council and voters assembly of the congregation to deal with their pastor and other called workers if they fall into error. The congregation must remove them from their office and from their membership in the congregation if they cling to false doctrine. The congregation may seek the advice and assistance of the district officials as they seek to carry out their duty in a scriptural way.

Doctrinal discipline at the district and synodical levels

According to the system of church government that WELS, its districts, and its congregations have adopted, the responsibility for dealing with congregations and called workers rests with the district president and his assistants. The district president in consultation with his assistants has the authority to suspend from membership in the synod any called workers or congregations who are clinging to error. If the suspended party feels that it has been treated unjustly, it may appeal to the district and synod, following procedures outlined in the synod and district constitution and bylaws.

Dealing with those who have been excluded from fellowship

Even when efforts to preserve a fellowship have failed, we are still ready to make every effort to restore the broken fellowship with a lost brother or sister. "In the name of the Lord Jesus Christ, we command you, brothers, to keep away from every brother who is idle and does not live according to the teaching you received from us. . . . Brothers, never tire of doing what is right. If anyone does not obey our instruction in this letter, take special note of him. Do not associate with him, in order that he may feel ashamed. Yet do not regard him as an enemy, but warn him as a brother" (2 Thessalonians 3:6,13-15). As the loving father in Jesus' parable was eager to regain his lost, prodigal son (Luke 15:11-24), so we are eager to regain a lost brother. In fact, our separation from him is part of our attempt to regain him. We hope this drastic warning will bring him to his senses so that he returns to the family of faith.

The command to separate from members whom we have had to place under discipline does not require us to have no social or business contacts with them of the sort we could have with any person of the world. But both before and after their removal from the congregation, members of the church may have to withdraw from social contacts that could give the impression that they approve of the offender's sin or dissent from the congregation's action against it (1 Corinthians 5:9-12). In a given case we should ask, "How can we give a clear testimony against the offender's impenitence? How can we sound a clear call to repentance?"

Working to extend fellowship

We also work to create new ties of fellowship whenever we preach the gospel to Christians and non-Christians. "The life appeared; we have seen it and testify to it, and we proclaim to you the eternal life, which was with the Father and has appeared to us. We proclaim to you what we have seen and heard, so that you also may have fellowship with us. And our fellowship is with the Father and with his Son, Jesus Christ" (1 John 1:2,3).

Our spiritual fellowship with God and with all believers is a gift that God has given us. Our outward fellowship with other Christians is likewise a gift, but it is also a responsibility. We must work hard to expand and preserve it, so that we may continue to "work together for the truth" (3 John 8) with all of those who hold to the truth.

Part II

THE HISTORY OF

THE DOCTRINE

OF CHURCH FELLOWSHIP

7

Fellowship in the Early Church and the Church of the Reformation

In the early church

In today's ecumenical climate it may seem that the WELS' fellowship and Communion practices are a strange innovation in the church since we are so out of step with the vast majority of the rest of Christendom. A survey of church history, however, reveals that the apostles' command to keep away from false teachers has directed the orthodox church's fellowship practices throughout all periods of its existence. The requirement of complete doctrinal unity as a basis for fellowship is not a newfangled notion, invented by WELS or the Synodical Conference. This has always been the orthodox church's practice. It is the modern indifference to doctrinal unity that is the departure from the established practice of the church.

Werner Elert's book *Eucharist and Church Fellowship in the First Four Centuries*[3] describes the practice that the early church learned from the apostles. He writes,

> The early church was never in doubt that unity in doctrine is a prerequisite of altar fellowship. No one who taught false doctrine might receive Holy Communion in an orthodox congregation (p. 109).

> There is no period in the early church when the question of the conditions and boundaries of church fellowship was not acute (p. 141).

But did this apply only to the leaders and teachers and not to the laity? We read,

> Never did the relations between two churches and their bishops provide for permitting the laity to receive the Sacrament while denying the clergy the privilege of officiating in it because church fellowship was somehow incomplete or because the congregations or their bishops were of different confessions or only in partial confessional agreement. There was either complete fellowship or none at all (p. 164).

> The modern theory that anybody may be admitted "as a guest" to the Sacrament in a church of a differing confession is unknown in the early church, indeed unthinkable (p. 175).

It appears that our practice of "closed Communion" has a long history. It is the practice to which the inspired apostolic writings have led us. It was also the practice of the early church.

The church of the Reformation

Luther took a strong stand against fellowship without complete agreement in all of the doctrines of Scripture. This conviction is expressed especially strongly in his comments on "A little yeast works through the whole batch of dough" (Galatians 5:9). This discussion is found in Luther's *Commentary on Galatians.* A few brief quotations are sufficient to represent his view:

> We are surely prepared to observe peace and love with all men, provided that they leave the doctrine of faith perfect and sound for us. If we cannot obtain this, it is useless for them to demand love from us. A curse on a love that is observed at the expense of the doctrine of faith! . . . When one [doctrine] is lost all are eventually lost, because they belong together and are held together by a common bond.[4]

> With the utmost rigor we demand that all the articles of Christian doctrine, both large and small—although we do not regard any of them as small—be kept pure and certain. This is supremely necessary. For this doctrine is our only light, which illumines and directs us and shows the way to heaven; if it is overthrown in one point, it must be overthrown completely. And when that happens, our love will not be of any use to us. We can be saved without love and concord with the Sacramentarians, but not without pure doctrine and faith. Otherwise we shall be happy to observe love and concord toward those who faithfully agree with us on all the articles of Christian doctrine. In fact, so far as we are concerned, we shall have peace with our enemies; and we shall pray for those who slander our doctrine and persecute us out of ignorance, but not with those who knowingly offend against one or more articles of Christian doctrine and against their conscience.[5]

From these statements it is clear that Luther believed that agreement in all doctrine is necessary for church fellowship. He also believed in what we would call "closed Communion."

> Although also the Gospel holds Christians together, the Lord's Supper does so still more. By attending it every Christian confesses publicly and for himself what he believes. There those who have a different faith part ways, and those meet who have the same faith, whose hope and heart toward the Lord are one. This is also the reason why the Sacrament has been called *communio* in Latin, a communion. And those who do not want to be of the same faith, doctrine, and life, as other Christians are, are called *excommunicatis*, people who are dissimilar in doctrine, words, understanding and life. Therefore these should not be tolerated in the group that has the same understanding; they would divide it and split it up.[6]

The orthodox teachers who followed Luther held similar views.

Friedrich Balduin (1575–1627), professor at Wittenberg, wrote,

> We should not confirm errorists in their error, which we do if we take part in their service. For in this way we give them the hope that finally we will come to agreement with them also in the remaining points. They will look upon our participation in their services as a sign that we thereby confess that we have separated from them without cause, since we in action approve of their worship.[7]

Johannes Quenstedt, one of the leading Lutheran theologians of the 17th century, said,

> An orthodox man should either abstain entirely from the sacred rites of unbelievers and heretics (especially the papists) or if he at one time or another wishes to attend or is required by official duties to attend, let him be careful not to give the appearance of secretly agreeing with them

. . . but rather let him in some way, either by words or signs, make clear his disagreement.[8]

The records of the theological faculty at Wittenberg are filled with discussions and opinions that the faculty prepared to assist individuals and congregations with difficult questions concerning church fellowship. Their detailed discussions of such matters as Communion practices, funerals, and the use of non-Lutheran musicians reveal that the orthodox Lutheran church was always very conscientious about a careful application of the principles of church fellowship.

During doctrinal talks between Lutheran, Reformed, and Catholic theologians held at Thorn, Poland, in 1645, each group held its own separate services before the sessions. Although the Reformed delegation was willing to join with the Catholics in opening and closing prayers since there was nothing offensive about the content of the prayers, the Lutheran delegation led by Johannes Huelsemann and Abraham Calov refused to participate in these joint prayers.[9]

The two principles that agreement in all doctrine is necessary for any fellowship and that the main purpose for refraining from fellowship with false teachers is to avoid giving support to error are not new in the church. They have always been maintained by the orthodox church.

8

The Split between
the Wisconsin and Missouri Synods

In every age the church has faced challenges to specific doctrines. The early church was challenged by attacks against the doctrines of the Trinity and Christ's deity. At the time of the Reformation, Rome's salvation by works and its hierarchical system of church government were the key issues. Today the battle to uphold the inspiration and inerrancy of Scripture is probably the most crucial issue. But the doctrinal controversy that has probably had the greatest emotional impact on the Wisconsin Synod in the 20th century was the long struggle with the Missouri Synod concerning the doctrine of church fellowship.

Although this book on church fellowship is not intended to be just a history book, we must take a close look at this long battle, since it was the most decisive event in the doctrinal development of our synod, and the issues at the center of this debate are still among the most critical issues confronting confessional Lutheranism today.

WELS and the LCMS in fellowship

For nearly a century, from 1868 until 1961, the Wisconsin Synod and the Missouri Synod were in church fellowship. In addition to enjoying altar and pulpit fellowship, they worked together in educational, charitable, and mission projects. Agreement in the doctrine of church fellowship was a key factor in bringing the two synods together. Disagreement in the doctrine of fellowship was the key factor in breaking them apart.

The Lutheran Church—Missouri Synod was organized in Chicago in 1847. The name *Missouri* derived from the "home base" of the synod's founders, a group of Saxon immigrants who had settled in and around St. Louis, Missouri, after fleeing from Germany in order to escape government pressure to compromise their Lutheran convictions.

The founder and first leader of the Missouri Synod was C. F. W. Walther, who quickly established himself as the leading spokesman for strong, confessional Lutheranism in America. His clear, firm doctrinal position strengthened confessional Lutheranism in America and, indeed, throughout the world.

The Wisconsin Synod was founded in 1850 by congregations in and around Milwaukee, Wisconsin. Under its first president, John Muehlhaeuser, the Wisconsin Synod represented a mild Lutheranism, committed to Scripture and the gospel, but with less emphasis on a strict Lutheran confession. Under the influence of German mission societies that did not regard the doctrinal differences between Lutherans and Reformed to be a hindrance to Communion fellowship, the Wisconsin Synod tolerated rather lax fellowship practices during its early days.

Such "union" mission societies in which Lutherans and Reformed worked together had been given impetus by the Prussian Union of 1817, when the king of Prussia had forced Lutherans and Reformed to join together in one church. The Wisconsin Synod's ties with these societies were very offensive to the Buffalo and Missouri Synods, since many of their members had fled Germany to escape the Prussian Union. Very soon, however, when John Bading became president in 1860 and Adolph Hoenecke emerged as its theological leader, the Wisconsin Synod broke its ties with the unionistic mission societies and embraced a sound, confessional Lutheranism.

Formation of the Synodical Conference

The Missouri Synod did not recognize the Wisconsin Synod as an orthodox synod with whom they could join in fellowship until 1868, after the Wisconsin Synod had developed a sound doctrinal position and practice concerning church fellowship. Once fellowship had been established, the two synods played key roles in founding the Synodical Conference of North America in 1872.

Throughout the history of the Synodical Conference, both the Wisconsin Synod and the Missouri Synod taught that agreement in all doctrines was necessary for church fellowship. Their shared belief is expressed in Thesis 7 of Walther's "Theses on Open Questions," on the basis of which the Wisconsin Synod and Missouri Synod established fellowship in 1868. It reads,

> No man has the privilege, and to no man may the privi-
> lege be granted, to believe and to teach otherwise than
> God has revealed in his Word, no matter whether it per-
> tains to primary or secondary fundamental articles of faith,
> to fundamental or nonfundamental doctrines, to matters
> of faith or of practice, to historical items or other matters
> subject to the light of reason, to important or seemingly
> unimportant matters.[10]

This position was opposed by the Lutheran church bodies that eventually formed the Lutheran Church in America (LCA) and the American Lutheran Church (ALC). These two churches are now merged into the Evangelical Lutheran Church in America (ELCA). These churches maintained that agreement in all doctrines is not needed as a basis for the practice of church fellowship. This was also the position of the so-called "moderates" (that is, liberals) who left the Missouri Synod in 1976 to form the Association of Evangelical Lutheran Churches (AELC), which also is now merged into ELCA. The ELCA maintains that unity of doctrine is not necessary for church fellowship, and it is seeking close ecumenical relationships with other Protestant churches and even with the Roman Catholic Church. It is considering practicing intercommunion with these churches in 1997.

During the early history of the Synodical Conference, the Missouri Synod and the Wisconsin Synod also agreed that unity of doctrine was a prerequisite for all forms of church fellowship, including joint prayer.[11] They put this common conviction into practice at the free conferences held during the early 1900s to discuss doctrine with the Ohio and Iowa Synods, which were not in fellowship with the Synodical Conference. At these meetings the Synodical Conference participants, including representatives of the Missouri Synod, objected to joint prayer. Their position is spelled out in Gerhard Friedrich Bente's essay "Why Can't We Establish and Maintain Common Prayer Services with Iowa and Ohio?"[12] The Missouri Synod's abandonment of this position during the 1930s and 1940s was a significant factor in the disagreement that led to the dissolution of the Synodical Conference.

Missouri begins to change fellowship doctrine and practice

A growing difference in the doctrine of church fellowship became apparent already in the 1930s, when the Missouri Synod entered fellowship discussions with the old American Lutheran Church. By 1938 the ALC was ready to declare full fellowship with Missouri in spite of remaining differences in "non-fundamental doctrines," since the ALC was convinced that "it is neither necessary nor possible to agree in all non-fundamental doctrines."[13] In the same year, the Missouri Synod declared that they sought *full* doctrinal agreement with the ALC and that more time and effort were needed before fellowship could be established, but they did so in a way that minimized the seriousness of the doctrinal differences that remained between the ALC and Missouri.[14]

In 1939 the Wisconsin Synod warned that genuine doctrinal agreement between the ALC and Missouri could not be achieved unless both churches adopted a single doctrinal statement that set forth the true doctrines and that rejected in clear, unmistakable terms all of the errors that had created a division between the two churches. WELS urged the LCMS to suspend fellowship discussions with the ALC since there was no genuine agreement between the

Missouri Synod and the ALC.[15] Nevertheless, the Missouri Synod continued to seek agreement with the ALC.

The issue of prayer fellowship

As these negotiations continued, the disagreement between WELS and the LCMS began to focus on prayer fellowship. As stated above, during the early decades of this century the two synods had agreed that there should be no joint prayers with leaders of churches with whom we were not in fellowship. The first stirrings of change occurred already in the mid-1920s.

An LCMS missionary in India, Adolph Brux, had written a lengthy essay defending his practice of prayer fellowship with missionaries in India who were not in fellowship with the Missouri Synod. Brux claimed that such Bible passages as Romans 16:17,18 did not apply to fellowship between Christians and that prayer fellowship may be practiced with all Christians. His fellow missionaries in India did not agree with his position, and his case was brought before the mission board. Brux was suspended from his call, but the dispute dragged on for many years. In the mid-1930s two Missouri Synod conventions sought to resolve the controversy by allowing Brux to be restored to his position if he withdrew charges of false doctrine against the Missouri Synod. These ambiguous settlement attempts failed because Brux maintained that he had not retracted his views, which were clearly contrary to the previous practice of the Missouri Synod. Brux ultimately resigned from the Missouri Synod. The irony was that within a few years Brux's position was accepted by the LCMS and two leading LCMS theologians who had played a role in the rejection of Brux's position became leaders of the LCMS' shift toward the Brux position.

The erosion of Missouri's position on prayer fellowship became more public after WELS objected to joint prayer between representatives of the LCMS and the ALC during their fellowship negotiations. At first the LCMS reaffirmed its position opposing joint prayer without doctrinal agreement. In 1940 the Missouri Synod declared, "Ordinarily, prayer fellowship involves church fellowship." The ALC responded, "We are convinced that prayer fellowship is wider than church fellowship, but we do not consider this difference as church-divisive."[16]

The 1941 and 1944 conventions of the Missouri Synod declared that no altar, pulpit, or prayer fellowship had been declared with the ALC and that none should be practiced by individuals or congregations of the synod, but the 1944 Missouri Synod convention undermined this resolution when it also resolved that joint prayer at intersynodical conferences does not violate the earlier resolution against joint prayer, provided that such prayer does not imply denial of truth or support of error.[17]

Although the resolution tried to limit the circumstances in which such prayer was allowed, the Missouri Synod had in effect adopted the ALC's position on prayer fellowship by its distinction between "prayer fellowship" and "joint prayer." This was a crucial turning point. Brux's position, which the LCMS had rejected only ten years before, was now the position of the LCMS. Although this resolution was intended to have a limited effect, it was an omen of things to come, and it paved the way for a wholesale erosion of Missouri's fellowship practices.

"A Statement" of the 44

"A Statement," a protest document signed by 44 prominent Missourians in 1945, was an endorsement of the

Brux-ALC fellowship principles and gave additional evidence of the change underway in Missouri. It insisted that "fellowship is possible without complete agreement in details of doctrine and practice."[18] William Arndt and Theodore Graebner, prominent LCMS theologians who had a role in the condemnation of Brux, were among the signers of "A Statement."

Especially ominous was the failure of the LCMS to discipline the signers despite the conviction of LCMS president John Behnken that the statement contained false doctrine. The signers of the statement were permitted to withdraw it from discussion without retracting it. The precedent set by this failure to exercise doctrinal discipline would have detrimental effects in the LCMS in subsequent years.

For several years the Missouri Synod wavered between the two views. In 1947 the synod declared it was not ready to enter fellowship with the ALC unless there was doctrinal agreement on the basis of a single clear document. It also issued some rather strong statements against prayer fellowship in situations in which doctrinal agreement had not yet been established. In spite of these declarations, however, worship services and joint church work with groups with whom the Missouri Synod was not in doctrinal agreement were becoming more and more common, and the participants remained undisciplined. Theodore Graebner, a prominent LCMS professor, produced a booklet advocating the position on prayer fellowship formerly advocated by Brux.[19] These mixed signals being sent out from the Missouri Synod made it difficult to determine their true position.

Continuing discussions between Missouri and the ALC

In 1944 the LCMS and the ALC had produced a joint "Doctrinal Affirmation" designed to be the one document that resolved the remaining doctrinal differences between Missouri and the ALC, but it was unsatisfactory. It was replaced by "The Common Confession" (1949–1952), but this document too proved unsatisfactory, since it did not specifically deal with the disputed points. Although this document stated that "a full and common obedience to the Holy Scriptures is an indispensable requisite for church fellowship," it did not show that such agreement really existed between Missouri and the ALC. There was no specific mention of prayer fellowship, and the document stressed that cooperation in proclaiming the gospel "should not be confused or identified with cooperation in externals."[20]

The 1950 LCMS convention approved a version of "The Common Confession" but took a strong stand against the newer, more lax position on prayer fellowship. It, however, refused to discipline the adherents of this position.

Further fellowship issues between WELS and the LCMS

By the 1950s WELS had become concerned about other practices of the LCMS that raised doubts about its fellowship principles. The two synods disagreed about the propriety of participating in the government's *military chaplaincy*. Missouri Synod pastors served in such positions. Since WELS believed this system entangled the chaplains in compromising fellowship positions, it served its members in the military by sending its own civilian chaplains.

In 1944 Missouri had abandoned its opposition to the *Boy Scouts*, permitting its congregations to sponsor troops. WELS objected to this change since the religious principles of the scouting movement undermine the truth of salvation by grace alone through Christ alone.

"Cooperation in externals" was the loophole that permitted the Missouri Synod to work together with the National Lutheran Council in providing spiritual care for their members in the military and in joint welfare work. Throughout the 1950s many additional examples of loose fellowship practices in the Missouri Synod became apparent.[21]

Breakup of the Synodical Conference

The Evangelical Lutheran Synod (ELS), a smaller member synod of the Synodical Conference, declared a suspension of fellowship with Missouri in 1955. The Wisconsin Synod continued to protest what was happening in Missouri and tried to reach a resolution of the growing differences through discussions of the Joint Union Committees. Throughout the 1950s there was an ongoing exchange of statements and counterstatements. In 1960 an impasse was declared after the LCMS issued the document "The Theology of Fellowship." Brux regarded this document as a vindication of the position he had advocated three decades earlier. The long process of deterioration had reached its sad conclusion.

This was the impasse: The Wisconsin Synod position was that there is only complete fellowship or none at all; the same scriptural principles cover every manifestation of a common faith (see WELS Theses, B, pp. 167-170 of this book). The Missouri Synod position was that some expressions of fellowship, such as joint prayer, could be undertaken without full agreement in doctrine. The propriety of joint prayer must be based on a consideration of the situation in which such prayer is offered, the character of the prayer itself, its purpose, and its probable effect on those who unite in the prayer."[22] The Wisconsin Synod broke fellowship with Missouri in 1961, and the Synodical Conference was in effect dissolved in 1963 by the withdrawal of the ELS and the Wisconsin Synod.

After the break with WELS, the Missouri Synod continued on its established course. In 1965 it approved membership in the ecumenical Lutheran Council in the USA (LCUSA). In 1967 the LCMS officially made the Brux position its own when it formally adopted a revised version of "The Theology of Fellowship." In 1969 it declared fellowship with the enlarged ALC. Throughout the 1960s the historical-critical method of studying the Bible, which allows human reason to pass judgment on Scripture, was firmly entrenched in the LCMS seminary at St. Louis. These actions demonstrated that WELS had not been overly pessimistic in its judgment of the LCMS which led to the break in fellowship.

This has been a rather long historical review, but its length should impress upon our minds the period from 1938 to 1961. In one respect this is a very long time. For almost 25 years the Wisconsin Synod had struggled with the issue of the Missouri Synod's changing doctrine of church fellowship. This interval indicates that WELS had not been hasty in the judgment that led it to break fellowship with the LCMS.

On the other hand, in the long view of church history, 25 years is not a very long time. It took less than a generation for the Missouri Synod to descend from its position as the strongest, clearest voice for confessional Lutheranism in the world to a middle-of-the-road position on fellowship that has created confusion and division in the ranks of confessional Lutheranism. This sad story illustrates the need to listen to the age-old warning "If you think you are standing firm, be careful that you don't fall" (1 Corinthians 10:12).

The divergence remains

Events in the Missouri Synod during the last 30 years, such as the departure of the liberal professors from Concordia Seminary in 1974, the breaking of fellowship between the LCMS and the ALC in 1981, and the unwillingness of Missouri to join in the merger that created the Evangelical Lutheran Church in America in 1988, have led some to ask whether the separation between the Missouri Synod and Wisconsin Synod can now be healed. Is the Missouri Synod returning to the position on church fellowship that once was the joint stand of all the synods of the Synodical Conference?

To their credit, in discussions with the ALC and LCA, and now with ELCA, the spokesmen of the Missouri Synod have continued to defend the scriptural principle that agreement in all doctrines is necessary for the practice of church fellowship. During a series of LCUSA study conferences between 1972 and 1977 on the unity of the church, the ALC and LCA representatives maintained that Article VII of the Augsburg Confession requires only "unity in the Gospel" as a basis for unity in the church and that "Gospel" is here to be limited to the narrow sense, namely, the promise of the forgiveness of sins. The LCMS representatives correctly maintained that the required "unity in the Gospel" must be understood in the wide sense of all doctrines, as is clearly indicated by the context of Article VII of the Augsburg Confession, which contrasts doctrines with ceremonies, and by the explanation in the Formula of Concord, Solid Declaration, X: 31, which calls for agreement in "doctrine and all its articles."

The report of a colloquium on "Unity in the Context of Theological Pluralism" provides another example of the approach to fellowship promoted by ELCA and its predecessor bodies. "We do not strive for Lutheran unity only by means of organizational union, although this may come in its own way, but primarily by means of pulpit and altar fellowship, including common witnessing and working. Thus we arrive at this Lutheran fellowship not only by doctrinal discussions and statements, but also by living in fellowship."[23] According to this view, pulpit and altar fellowship are not a result of doctrinal unity, but a stepping stone toward a vague doctrinal consensus. The practice of fellowship without prior agreement in doctrine is seen as a tool for increasing fellowship ties even though attempts at reaching doctrinal unity have proven futile.

In 1978 the ALC demonstrated the widening gap between itself and Missouri on fellowship matters when it abandoned the long-standing rule "Lutheran altars for Lutherans only" in its new "Statement on Communion Practices."[24] This document, also approved by the LCA, approved open Communion in Lutheran churches and participation by Lutherans at non-Lutheran Communion services, since all Christians are members of one universal church. The ELCA's present movement toward intercommunion with Episcopalians, other Reformed, and even Roman Catholics are simply further steps in the same process.

The natural outcome of the approach to fellowship advocated by the ELCA is indicated by the "convergence" on the doctrine of justification that Lutheran and Catholic theologians adopted in 1983. The participants discovered enough "unity in the Gospel" between Lutherans and Catholics to recommend fellowship and at least limited sharing of the Lord's Supper between these two.[25] The Lutheran and Catholic representatives agreed that we are saved by grace through faith, but this is nothing new, since Catholics have always believed this. The problem is that Catholics refuse to accept the scriptural truth that we are saved by faith *alone* and not by works. The critical difference of doctrine that led to separation at the time of the Reformation still exists, but liberal Catholics and Lutherans are attempting to paper it over with ambiguous agreements.

To their credit, official Missouri representatives have attempted to disassociate themselves from the extremes of their LCUSA partners in fellowship matters. This testimony has apparently not been without effect, since LCUSA-ELCA Lutherans have occasionally expressed bitterness over Missouri's pointed refusal to practice full altar and pulpit fellowship with them.

Missouri, however, has not made notable progress toward returning to the scriptural position of requiring agreement in all doctrines of Scripture as the prerequisite for all expressions of church fellowship. LCUSA ceased to exist when the ALC and LCA merged into ELCA in 1988, but the LCMS continues in a limited fellowship relationship with ELCA, which is similar to the relationship that existed under LCUSA. Theologians of the Missouri Synod still join in joint prayer and devotions with theologians of ELCA in spite of the major doctrinal differences that separate them.

In 1981 the Missouri Synod's Commission on Theology and Church Relations issued a document called "The Nature and Implications of the Concept of Fellowship." This document maintained that declarations of pulpit and altar fellowship between church bodies that are agreed in doctrine and practice is the proper way of establishing church fellowship. Three other approaches to church fellowship were rejected: (1) the "conciliar model" of church fellowship promoted by the World Council of Churches, in which local churches work toward organizational unity without fixed doctrinal standards for establishing unity; (2) the "reconciled diversity" advocated by the Lutheran World Federation, in which churches practice fellowship despite unresolved doctrinal differences; and (3) "selective fellowship," which has been suggested by many in the Missouri Synod, according to which each local congregation decides which congregations and individuals it wishes to practice fellowship with.

Unfortunately, this stand is immediately weakened by this statement:

> Through the use of the word "fellowship" almost exclusively to refer to a formal altar and pulpit fellowship relationship established between two church bodies on the basis of agreement in the confession of the faith, some have been given the impression that no fellowship relationship other than the spiritual unity in the body of Christ can or should exist among members of Christian churches not in altar and pulpit fellowship. The fact that the LC-MS is closer doctrinally to a church body which at least formally accepts the Scriptures and the Lutheran Confessions than to those denominations which do not is often obscured by the "all or nothing" approach that frequently accompanies ecclesiastical declarations of altar and pulpit fellowship.[26]

This statement is clearly intended to be a public rejection of WELS' "unit concept" of church fellowship. This statement and the rest of the document advocate the position that although complete doctrinal agreement is needed for formal altar and pulpit fellowship, it is not necessary for other expressions of fellowship such as joint prayer. That this is indeed the intention of the statement is indicated by subsequent actions of the leadership of the Missouri Synod.

In response to the decision to form ELCA, President Ralph Bohlmann of the LCMS delivered a message to the conventions of the AELC, the ALC, and the LCA. In it Bohlmann repeated the Missouri Synod's position that "fellowship and external unity in the church must be based on agreement in doctrine and all its articles, as well as the right use of the Holy Sacraments" and cited this conviction as the reason that the LCMS would not be entering the new church, nor would it enter official sharing of the Lord's Supper with it.

Nevertheless, Bohlmann went on to say, "We in the LC-MS congratulate you on your efforts to form a new church body, and we pray God's blessing upon you as you carry out the arduous tasks associated with its formation. Whether you are structured in one church body or in several, we look forward to continuing fellowship and cooperation in inter-Lutheran agencies and in other civic and churchly activities and associations."[27] It is hardly appropriate for confessional Lutherans to extend congratulations for the establishment of a new Lutheran church based on the elimination of scriptural inerrancy from its constitution.

The official Missouri Synod policy is no altar and pulpit fellowship without doctrinal agreement, but fellowship in "externals." The LCMS tendency toward artificial distinctions, such as distinguishing between prayer fellowship and joint prayer appears to have gotten worse rather than better, as can be seen in the practice of distinguishing between worship services, which require full fellowship, and convocations or rallies, which do not, even if they include many elements of worship.

In 1983 the Missouri Synod's Council of Presidents approved a set of guidelines on joint worship.[28] This document requires all members of the Missouri Synod to practice joint worship only with those with whom the LCMS has declared pulpit and altar fellowship. They may, however, participate in joint celebrations, concerts, convocations, rallies, and conferences if there is no sermon or sacrament and the clergy are not dressed in vestments. Among the valid reasons for such events are thanksgiving for the doctrinal heritage of Lutheranism, prayer for greater doctrinal unity, and encouragement of appropriate cooperative efforts in externals. Thanksgiving, prayer, and encouragement are certainly expressions of faith and fellowship. To make matters worse, the document appeals to synod positions and policies, rather than to Scripture. Thus, there is no official evidence that Missouri is ready to deal seriously with the differences on fellowship principles that continue to separate our synods.

This fellowship practice of the LCMS has been called levels of fellowship or degrees of fellowship since it does not require complete agreement in all doctrine for all expressions of fellowship, but requires only different levels or degrees of doctrinal agreement for different levels of fellowship activity. President Bohlmann expressed it this way: "Complete agreement on confessional doctrine is neither possible nor necessary for every inter-Christian and inter-denominational action. Expressions of Christian unity should be proportionate to the measure of consensus in confessing the Biblical Gospel we enjoy with the Christians involved. Although this point has seldom been articulated in official synodical documents, it has in fact been practiced by the Missouri Synod for many years."[29] In a video designed to promote the "levels of fellowship" concept in the LCMS, President Bohlmann rejected the Wisconsin Synod position by name.

To make matters worse, many in Missouri go far beyond the degree of unionistic practices that the official position condones. The widespread practice of open Communion and participation in ecumenical services has gone undisciplined. Some do this knowingly and persistently, in deliberate defiance of their synod's position, and yet remain undisciplined.

Christians do have a responsibility to admonish weak brothers, but those who publicly defy the synod's position and declare that their own position is the correct scriptural position can no longer be considered weak brothers. In a fellowship where diversity of doctrine and practice is tolerated and abounds, it becomes impossible to fulfill the duty to correct weak brothers. Where difference of doctrine is tolerated, each position considers itself to be the strong one and all other positions to be the weak ones. The ability to deal scripturally both with weak brothers and with those who prove themselves to be persistent errorists is lost. This is the problem in Missouri today. Until this situation is corrected, it will loom as a huge barrier to any possibility of reestablishing fellowship between our two synods.

Concerned voices are still speaking out in the Missouri Synod. In 1995, for example, the LCMS convention reaffirmed the synod's opposition to open Communion. Nevertheless, humanly speaking, it does not appear likely that Missouri will soon return to the position on fellowship that we once shared with them in the Synodical Conference, either in theory or in practice. There are as yet no signs that those who practice open Communion will be disciplined.

Al Barry, the current president of the LCMS, who was elected at least in part because of his conservative position, has spoken in defense of closed Communion. Nevertheless, Barry defends the LCMS distinction between joint prayer and prayer fellowship.

Justification for this position is often sought in the fact that the free conferences called by C. F. W. Walther between 1856 and 1859 were opened with prayer although the synods represented at the free conferences were not in doctrinal agreement. This, however, ignores the critical difference between those early inter-Lutheran conferences and later conferences with theologians from ELCA and its predecessor bodies during the early 1900s, the 1930s, the 1960s, and today.

The conferences during the 1850s were for individuals who were "united in faith" and who accepted Lutheran doctrine as expressed in the Augsburg Confession without reservation. This was a period when confessional Lutherans in America were groping to find each other and when a clear understanding of the practice of fellowship was still being solidified. It was not yet clear that any of the participants in these conferences were persistent errorists. After things were sorted out and the position of the various synods had been clarified, the situation was much different. After it became clear that predecessor synods of the ALC and ELCA, such as the Ohio and Iowa Synods, rejected the doctrinal position of the Synodical Conference, representatives of the Synodical Conference no longer practiced joint prayer with them. The representatives of the ALC in the 1930s and the representatives of ELCA today are spokesmen for synods that have taken a public stand in opposition to the teachings of the Bible. With such there can be no fellowship.

There has been no interest from the LCMS in recent years in discussing these issues with WELS. This is not necessarily bad, since it may be best for the LCMS to first establish internal agreement on this issue. There is, therefore, at present no reason to be optimistic that this dispute can be resolved in the near future. WELS can only continue to give its testimony and to pray that, through the power of his Word and Spirit, the Lord will restore the agreement in the scriptural principles that the two synods once shared.

Church and ministry and the roles of men and women in the church are two other doctrines that cause unresolved differences between WELS and the LCMS. These issues would also have to be considered as part of any efforts to reestablish doctrinal agreement between the LCMS and WELS as a basis for a restoration of fellowship. There is no indication that these issues can be resolved in the near future.

9

The Split between WELS and the CLC Concerning Church Fellowship

Although the Wisconsin Synod had been protesting the changes in the Missouri Synod's position on fellowship for nearly 25 years before it broke fellowship with Missouri in 1961, some members of WELS thought the break was made too soon. Another large group, however, was equally convinced that the Wisconsin Synod was tardy in making the break. Some of them were so strongly convinced of this that they left the Wisconsin Synod and started a new church body, the Church of the Lutheran Confession (CLC). The disagreement between WELS and the CLC concerning the application of the doctrine of church fellowship constituted a second test of WELS' convictions concerning this doctrine.

With hindsight it is easy to argue that the Wisconsin Synod was slow in catching on to what was happening in the Missouri Synod. Couldn't people see that the Missouri Synod had abandoned its old position on fellowship? This, however, was not so clear in the midst of the smoke of battle.

In 1938 when the trouble began to become public, Missouri was regarded as the unquestioned champion of Lutheran orthodoxy in the world. It had been only six years since the LCMS had adopted the *Brief Statement*, a document that the Wisconsin Synod approved of wholeheartedly. During the next two decades, there were enough zigzags in Missouri's position to leave observers wondering what their real position was. The difficulty was compounded by the fact that the Missouri Synod was a house divided. It is relatively easy to determine the position and attitude of an individual or a small group, but how does one determine whether a large group scattered throughout the country is made up of weak brothers or persistent errorists? Which of the conflicting views is representative of the group? When is it clear that admonition has been heard and rejected by the erring group? Disagreement concerning these questions led to the departure of the members of the CLC from the Wisconsin Synod during the 1950s.

By 1952 the prospects of resolving the dispute with Missouri seemed so bleak that WELS delegates at the meeting of the Synodical Conference declared themselves to be in a state of protesting fellowship against the Missouri Synod. The 1953 WELS convention received a recommendation that it declare its fellowship with Missouri at an end. The convention, however, instead accepted the substance of the floor committee report that expressed approval for our delegates' declaration of a protesting fellowship in the pre-vious year and requested that the 1954 meeting of the Synodical Conference devote all its sessions to efforts to prevent the impending break. The 1954 Synodical Con-ference meeting, however, only demonstrated once more that the conference was very divided. The events of these years demonstrate, however, that the Wisconsin Synod was making every possible effort to prevent the breach.

The actions of the 1955 WELS convention, which fol-lowed this disappointing meeting of the Synodical Confer-ence, became a bone of contention between WELS and the CLC. The ELS had already suspended fellowship with Missouri. Now the 1955 WELS convention was faced with a dilemma. On the one hand, the situation that had pro-duced the strong WELS protest in 1953 had not gotten any better in the meanwhile. If the 1955 WELS conven-tion failed to act, it could undercut the strong testimony that had been given by the 1953 convention. Many dele-gates feared that WELS would be guilty of the very union-ism it was condemning in Missouri if it failed to break fel-lowship with Missouri immediately.

On the other hand, it was difficult for delegates to the 1955 convention to declare decisively that the Missouri Synod had rejected the warning delivered by the 1953 WELS convention, since the Missouri Synod held con-ventions only every three years and had not met since the WELS protest had been delivered in 1953.

This dilemma led to the much debated 1955 resolu-tions of WELS. The convention unanimously adopted a preamble that rebuked Missouri's unionism and declared it to be the cause for a break in relations. But then, by a 2-1 vote, it decided to postpone a final vote on breaking fellowship. The convention would recess and would reconvene after hearing from the 1956 Missouri Synod convention. Some 50 delegates formally protested this postponement.

In 1956 the Missouri Synod declared that the unsatisfactory "Common Confession" would no longer function as a union document between the LCMS and the ALC and expressed its gratitude for WELS' concerns and admonitions. In response to these perceived overtures, the recessed convention of WELS, which reconvened in 1956, again postponed final action and endorsed a meeting of LCMS and WELS representatives with theologians from overseas sister churches who hoped to serve as mediators in a final attempt to resolve the dispute. The 1957 WELS convention was sharply divided on whether an immediate termination of fellowship was called for. The floor committee strongly endorsed a break of fellowship, but after long debate the motion was defeated, 61-77.

Many felt this action was a sinful failure to break with persistent errorists. Others were convinced it was patient dealing with weak brothers who had not yet rejected our testimony, since the discussion of fellowship with the representatives of the LCMS had not yet been completed. The opinion prevailed that the work of the new committee established by the four synods of the Synodical Conference had not yet been completed.[30]

We have already seen that WELS finally broke fellowship with Missouri in 1961, after the additional efforts at reconciliation proposed by the 1957 WELS convention failed to resolve the issue.

WELS' failure to break fellowship in 1955 and 1957, however, became a key factor in the departure of the CLC from WELS. Already in 1953 there had been some departures from WELS as a result of its failure to break fellowship with Missouri. This exodus increased after 1955 and 1957. In 1960 these people, along with others who had departed from the ELS for similar reasons, formed the Church of the Lutheran Confession with about 60 pastors and 9,000 members.

WELS did not and does not condemn those who departed from WELS because their consciences did not permit them to remain in fellowship with the Missouri Synod. But after WELS broke fellowship with Missouri, there was hope that the break with the CLC could be mended, since the cause of the division had now been removed. However, all attempts to remove this division over a 30-year period have proved unsuccessful.

Over the years, the sticking point has been whether there is a difference between WELS and the CLC in the doctrine of fellowship, or whether there is only disagreement about the way WELS had applied the doctrine to the termination of fellowship with the Missouri Synod. In other words, did WELS fail to break fellowship with the Missouri Synod in 1955 and 1957 because it had a faulty doctrine of fellowship, which allowed continued fellowship with persistent errorists, or was the delay due to a difference of opinion about whether the Missouri Synod had heard and rejected our admonition, thereby justifying the conclusion that it was persisting in its error in spite of admonition?

Those who have felt that there was a difference of doctrine between WELS and the CLC have usually pointed in one of two directions in identifying that difference. Some individuals in WELS have identified that difference as a failure on the part of the CLC to allow for admonition before the termination of fellowship with an erring church. Individuals in the CLC have regularly identified the difference as a willingness on the part of WELS to remain in fellowship with an erring church body, even after it had been identified as persisting in its error.

But when representatives of the two church bodies met, the CLC representatives claimed that their church does allow for admonition, and WELS representatives have denied that their synod allows continued fellowship with persistent errorists. As a result, WELS representatives who met with the CLC consistently concluded that there was no doctrinal difference, but a difference of application and differing interpretations of the events of 1955 and 1957.

This belief that there was initially no difference of doctrine was supported by the recollection that Professor E. Reim, a prominent founder of the CLC, had continued to practice fellowship with a WELS congregation for two years after his resignation as president of our seminary, an action he surely would not have taken if he had believed there was a difference of doctrine. (A 1973 WELS convention resolution referring to a "doctrinal difference" was an anomaly since it did not accurately reflect the wording of the report submitted by the WELS commission that had met with the CLC.) The CLC, however, has continued to claim that a difference in doctrine divided the two synods.

For this reason, the most recent talks between WELS, the ELS, and the CLC, held between 1987 and 1990, focused on the role of admonition in termination of fellowship with an erring church body. At the outset of the discussions a CLC representative observed that in the years before 1961, there was much confusion and unclarity on all sides. In a joint statement, drafted in

April of 1990 after much study and discussion, the representatives of the three churches agreed with the following statement:

> Admonition continues until the erring individual or group either repents of its error and turns away from it or until it shows itself to be persistent in its error by adhering to it in its public doctrine and practice, by demanding recognition for it, or by making propaganda for it and trying to persuade others of it.[31]

Both sides thus agreed on the necessity of admonition before the termination of fellowship. Both parties also accepted the following statement on the limited duration of the admonition:

> The imperative *ekklinate* calls for a clean break of fellowship with those who persistently adhere to error. When it has been ascertained that a person or church body is causing divisions and offenses . . . by teaching contrary to Holy Scripture, the directive to avoid is as binding as any word addressed to us by our Savior in his holy Word. Pleading a debt of love dare not serve as an excuse for putting off a break in fellowship with those who have shown themselves to be not weak brethren but persistent errorists. . . . We reject the view that the decision to continue or discontinue admonition and proceed to avoid is to be made on the basis of a subjective human judgment or conjecture about the possible outcome of the admonition. . . . We reject the view that permits the use of human judgment to prolong fellowship with persistent errorists as contrary to the principles of Scripture.[32]

The subsequent acceptance of this doctrinal statement by the doctrinal committees of all three synods in their 1990 spring meetings led the WELS Commission on Inter-Church Relations to conclude once again that there was no difference of doctrine between WELS and the CLC.

There was, however, a new difficulty to be resolved. Near the end of the meeting that had drafted the joint statement, the CLC representatives proposed an addition to the statement—a preamble that referred to the existence of a doctrinal difference between WELS and the CLC. Since this seemed to contradict the substance of the statement itself, which revealed no doctrinal difference between the synods, this preamble was not acceptable to WELS and the ELS.

To deal with the misgivings raised by the CLC representatives, WELS representatives later suggested a different preamble, which included these words: "This Joint Statement, therefore, when accepted by our three church bodies, supersedes any and every previous statement that might be or might appear to be in conflict with this document. Any and all such conflicting or possibly conflicting statements are herewith disavowed."[33]

When our commission asked the CLC what the basis was for their renewed assertion that there is a doctrinal difference between the CLC and WELS, the CLC did not provide a direct answer, but merely provided copies of old documents. The 1992 CLC convention reaffirmed the claim of a doctrinal difference. Following this impasse, the CLC broke off discussions with WELS, and another effort at reconciliation had ended in failure.

Recently, several documents from CLC sources have attempted to provide a basis for the claim that such a doctrinal difference exists. In response to a request from a CLC congregation that the CLC state clearly what the doctrinal difference with WELS is, the CLC's 1994 convention adopted the following statements:

Whereas, the WELS, having already "marked" the LC-MS in 1955 as a causer of divisions and offenses nevertheless at its 1959 convention adopted the following principle on the Termination of Church Fellowship: "Termination of church fellowship is called for when you have reached the conviction that admonition is of no further avail and that the erring brother or church body demands recognition of its error" and

Whereas, the CLC holds to the scriptural principle set forth in its official publication, "Concerning Church Fellowship," which says: "We further believe and teach that suspension of an established fellowship is to take place when it has been ascertained that a person or group is causing divisions and offenses through a false position in doctrine or practice" therefore, be it

Resolved, that we let the doctrinal contrast between these two official statements from the respective church bodies stand as our answer to the memorial of Holy Spirit congregation of Albuquerque, NM.[34]

It is as though the CLC-WELS-ELS meetings and agreement of 1987–1990 had never occurred. The WELS position is misrepresented by the detachment of a single sentence from its context, and the CLC statement does not even mention the role of admonition, which was the focal point of the discussions. ·

A recent essay by a leader of the CLC summarizes the WELS position in this way: "It is wrong to avoid . . . only when we come to some sort of subjective judgment that admonition will *never* be heeded (as the WELS and ELS falsely teach) [Emphasis added]."[35] This is a distortion of the WELS position. We do maintain that we must determine whether our admonition has been heard and rejected before we break fellowship, but not that we must judge that our admonition will never be heeded.

A 1994 conference essay by a CLC pastor summarizes the WELS-ELS position as "mark, admonish, and avoid" false teachers.[36] We could accept this summary if it is understood to mean: (1) "mark," that is, "watch out for" false teachers; (2) "admonish" them when you spot them; and (3) "avoid" them if they reject your admonition. The same essay summarizes the CLC position as "mark and avoid," with no mention of admonition. This seeming revival of the old CLC interpretation of "mark and avoid" gives new credibility to the old opinion that the CLC departs from Scripture by allowing no room for admonition before a break of fellowship. This CLC position seems to be based on a misinterpretation of the Greek word translated "mark" in the King James Version of Romans 16:17. Some CLC writers seem to think this means, "identify false teachers and immediately avoid them." But in King James English "mark" does not mean "identify" or "brand." It means "watch out for." Romans 16:17 does not deal with the role of admonition. This must be determined from other passages.

The 1994 CLC essay goes on to state that one basis for the CLC's assertion that WELS has a different doctrine than the CLC is that WELS has never officially adopted the 1990 Joint Statement approved by WELS and CLC representatives. But this happened because the CLC broke off the talks before a mutually acceptable preamble could be added to the document to satisfy their request. When the CLC refused further discussions, there was no reason to present the statement to a WELS convention for adoption since there was no agreement between the synods.[37]

It is sad that the recent talks, which began so promisingly, failed to produce concrete steps toward removing the division between WELS and the ELS on the one hand and the CLC on the other. It is doubly sad that the CLC spokesmen are ignoring the Joint Statement that was accepted by all parties to the negotiations and basing allegations of a doctrinal difference between WELS and the CLC on a caricature of the WELS position that WELS representatives cannot accept as an accurate summary of their view.

10

Working toward the CELC

The many efforts made by WELS during the 30 years since the break with Missouri to preserve and extend our fellowship throughout the world prove that strict fellowship practices do not lead to isolationism.

For 30 years the Evangelical Lutheran Confessional Forum has been meeting regularly to preserve and strengthen ties between WELS and the Evangelical Lutheran Synod, which had been our sister synod already in the former Synodical Conference.

From 1964 to 1970 the WELS Commission on Inter-Church Relations sponsored an annual "free conference" to provide individual Lutherans who were concerned about the doctrinal deterioration of their churches with a forum for mutual strengthening so that ultimately they could come to full unity of doctrine and practice.

In 1971 WELS established fellowship with the Federation for Authentic Lutheranism (FAL), a group of congregations that left the LCMS for confessional reasons. In 1975 FAL disbanded, and most of its congregations joined WELS or the ELS.

In 1995 WELS and the ELS established fellowship with the Lutheran Confessional Synod, which was founded as a place of refuge for congregations leaving ELCA for confessional reasons.

Overseas, WELS established fellowship in 1974 with the Lutheran Confessional Church (often called the LBK from its Swedish initials), a church formed by dedicated Christians who left the liberal Lutheran state churches of Sweden and Norway for confessional reasons.

The other fellowship efforts of WELS since 1961 have been directed toward ultimately gathering all the churches throughout the world that are in fellowship with us into an international organization of confessional Lutherans, the Confessional Evangelical Lutheran Conference. But first, there was a significant problem to overcome.

When we broke fellowship with Missouri in 1961, both WELS and the LCMS were in fellowship with many other Lutheran churches throughout the world. Many of them were mission churches of the LCMS; some were WELS missions; at least one was a result of joint WELS-LCMS mission work through the Synodical Conference; some were independent churches. Since WELS and the LCMS were no longer in doctrinal agreement, it would have been a violation of scriptural principles for these churches to stay in fellowship with both the LCMS and WELS. By and large, the mission churches naturally stayed with their mother synod, but prolonged efforts were necessary to clarify the fellowship relations between WELS and several of the independent churches.

WELS representatives made long journeys, held many discussions, and exchanged extensive correspondence in their efforts to preserve our fellowship with Lutheran free churches in Germany, France and Belgium, England, Denmark, Finland, and South Africa after those fellowship ties had been placed into jeopardy by the breakup of the Synodical Conference. These efforts ultimately proved unsuccessful, since, with one exception in Germany, these churches chose to remain in fellowship with the LCMS.

WELS' experience in Germany was a mixture of sorrow and joy. In 1972 several of the confessional Lutheran churches in West Germany merged into the Independent Evangelical Lutheran Church, commonly called SELK from its German initials. In 1973 a meeting in Mequon, Wisconsin, established doctrinal agreement between WELS and SELK representatives, but SELK repudiated the agreement reached by its representatives. This made it impossible for us to establish fellowship with SELK and forced us to suffer the loss of fellowship of one of our mission churches, which joined SELK in 1976.

In East Germany the Evangelical Lutheran Free Church (ELFC), which had been in fellowship with both Missouri and Wisconsin since the 19th century, was largely cut off from developments in the West by the Berlin Wall. When East Germany became more accessible again, it became possible to renew efforts to clarify our fellowship ties with the ELFC. The ELFC was in fellowship with both WELS and the LCMS, but the latter two were not in fellowship with each other, a situation called triangular fellowship. The result of the new discussions was that the ELFC broke its ties with the Missouri Synod and with the European confessional churches that had remained in fellowship with Missouri, and it reestablished a strong active fellowship with WELS. The resolution of this triangular fellowship, which had been long delayed by the Berlin Wall, opened the way for the establishment of the Confessional Evangelical Lutheran Conference, since there were now no more churches in contradictory fellowships with both WELS and the LCMS.

In 1993 the Confessional Evangelical Lutheran Conference was founded in Oberwesel, Germany, with 13 member churches from the United States, Germany, Sweden and Norway, Finland, Puerto Rico, Mexico, Australia, Cameroon, Nigeria, Zambia, Malawi, and Japan. We hope that this conference will continue to grow so that it will be a source of strength and encouragement to confessional Lutherans throughout the world.

The WELS Commission on Inter-Church Relations regularly receives inquiries from confessional Lutherans throughout the world. It does everything it can to assist them in developing a sound confessional position and practice.

The purpose of this account of the WELS' fellowship efforts during the last 30 years is to demonstrate our willingness to do everything we can to "work together for the truth" with confessional Lutherans throughout the world.

Part III

THE APPLICATIONS

OF THE PRINCIPLES

OF CHURCH FELLOWSHIP

11

Basic Applications of the Principles of Church Fellowship

Review of the biblical principles

We will now apply the scriptural principles of church fellowship that we studied in Part I of this book to various situations in the life of the church. Before we consider these applications, however, we must briefly restate the basic principles of church fellowship.

Christian fellowship refers to the spiritual fellowship that we have with God and with all believers through faith in Christ as our Savior. We cherish these fellowships as a great blessing. But here, when we speak about practicing the principles of *church fellowship*, we are referring to every activity in which Christians join together with other members of the visible church to give joint expression to their faith.

Since we cannot see the faith in people's hearts, we must determine whether we can practice fellowship with an individual or a group by comparing their confession of faith with Scripture. If individuals or groups agree concerning all of the doctrines of Scripture, they should practice church fellowship together. If they do not agree in doctrine, they should not practice church fellowship with each other.

The unit concept

We have seen that church fellowship must be dealt with as an undivided whole in two different respects. First, when the doctrines of Scripture are being discussed to determine if two groups may practice fellowship together, all doctrine must be dealt with as a unit. Since all the teachings of Scripture have the same divine authority, and we have no right to add anything to them nor to subtract anything from them, the practice of church fellowship must be based on agreement in *all* of the doctrines of Scripture.

Second, the various activities that may express church fellowship must be dealt with as a unit. Since various ways of expressing church fellowship (such as joint mission work, celebration of the Lord's Supper, exchange of pulpits, transfers of membership, and joint prayer) are merely different ways of expressing the same fellowship of faith, *all* expressions of church fellowship require the same degree of doctrinal agreement, namely, agreement in all of the doctrines of Scripture.

Some guidelines in applying the principles

Before we consider specific applications of the principles of fellowship, we will consider some general guidelines that should govern our attitude and actions as we wrestle with specific cases.

1. Before we tackle tough cases, we should be sure that all parties in the discussion understand and agree with the scriptural principles as discussed above. We cannot make sound applications without a clear understanding of the principles. This means that we will constantly be studying the principles in Scripture, not simply receiving them by tradition.

2. We must be careful that we do not allow difficult cases to establish or modify the principles. We may not let feelings, emotions, or human reason pressure us into a particular application and then reshape our principles to condone our action.

3. We must guard against allowing specific applications or historical precedents to become rigid rules that govern all similar cases. We must evaluate each case in the light of the scriptural principles.

4. We must remember that there are hard cases (cases of casuistry) in which it is difficult to determine which scriptural principle applies. For example, is it still time to warn, or is it now time to avoid? In such cases, like-minded Christians may not reach the same conclusion at the same time. We should be careful not to pass hasty judgment on decisions that fellow Christians have made in such difficult cases. We may not know all the circumstances that led them to their decision. We should patiently listen to their explanations.

5. When we are faced with such a hard case, we should seek the advice of fellow Christians and explain the reasons for our actions to those who are concerned about them.

6. We should recognize that exceptional cases may lead us to depart from our normal practice, but we should be on

guard that exceptions are not used to undermine the principles.

7. We must constantly balance two responsibilities: to patiently admonish the weak and to promptly separate from those who cling to error. How can we determine if we are dealing with weak brothers and sisters or with persistent adherents of false doctrine? We can determine this only by examining their confession. What do they say? What do they do? Does their confession contradict Scripture? Are they willing to accept instruction and correct their errors? Do they reject correction and hold to their error? Are they making propaganda for their error?

In this process we must guard against two types of judging the heart: We cannot say of the penitent, "I don't believe his retraction. He is a hypocrite." We cannot say of the one who holds to error, "I think he's really sincere. Maybe he'll change his mind someday." We can judge only by the person's confession. If he corrects his error, we may remain in fellowship with him. If he does not, we must separate from him.

8. We must pray for patience and humility in dealing with the weak. We ask God to free us from pride, impatience, and legalistic tendencies, which may make us unwilling to bear with the weak. But showing love for the weak does not mean that we will be weak in acting against error, even when our action may not be fully understood by those who have a weak understanding of the principles.

9. We must be careful that our patience in dealing with the weak does not become a source of offense and confusion to other Christians who get the impression that we are condoning the error. We can guard against this by reporting the status of our dealings with the errorist to our brothers and sisters in the faith.

10. We must pray for courage and decisiveness in dealing with the adherents of error. We ask God to take away any timidity or desire for the approval of men, which may make us hesitant to testify clearly against error or may make us willing to yield to false teachers and their followers (Ezekiel 2:3-7; 3:3-8).

11. We should be indignant when God's Word is twisted in support of all sorts of false teaching and shameful conduct (Psalm 119:129-144).

12. When we must refuse to practice fellowship with adherents of false teaching, we should be sure that all parties are aware of the specific commands of God's Word that make it impossible for us to work together with these people. God's doctrine is at stake here, not ours. We express our concern for doctrine each time we pray "hallowed be your name." When we practice the principles of church fellowship, we are obeying the Second Commandment, which teaches us to honor God's name.

13. We must not regard our responsibility to practice the principles of church fellowship as a burden or a handicap, but as a privilege and an opportunity. Here is an opportunity to show love for God and for our neighbor. Here is an opportunity to suffer for the truth if it is God's will that we do so (1 Peter 4:12-16).

14. Above all, remember that these are not our principles of church fellowship; they are God's principles revealed in Holy Scripture. Human judgment cannot determine the principles. They are established by God's Word. But human judgment must evaluate each situation to see which principles apply at a particular moment. As with any application of law and gospel, the proper application of the principles of church fellowship requires life-long study and practice. We pray that God gives us the

willingness and the wisdom to apply these principles faithfully.

****

****

Applications of the principles

The double line above the preceding subtitle has a very specific purpose. It emphasizes the importance of maintaining a clear distinction between the principles set forth in Scripture and our applications of them. It is important that we not raise our applications to a level of equality with the scriptural principles.

The ease or difficulty of making an application may vary. Some of our fellowship practices are simply further instances of applications already made in Scripture. For example, Scripture states very clearly that we may not give financial support to false teachers, so we obviously should not give money to heterodox churches.

In other cases we have no clear precedents in Scripture since we are dealing with institutions or situations that did not exist in New Testament times. For example, Scripture provides us with no specific criteria for determining who can attend our Lutheran elementary schools.

Sometimes cases are very clear-cut. We obviously cannot let a false teacher preach in our congregations. At other times we are confronted with situations in which two or more biblical principles seem to be in tension. We have a responsibility to deal patiently with the weak person who has fallen into error, but we have an equal responsibility to avoid giving offense to other weak Christians who might be misled by his error.

In the following discussion we will begin with more clear-cut applications that are very similar to situations discussed in Scripture. The second part of the discussion considers more difficult cases, which we call cases of casuistry. This part of the discussion is not intended to provide a rule book or a set of legal precedents for dealing with all similar cases in the future. The aim is to provide examples of how to deal with such cases in an evangelical way. In two situations that appear to be quite similar in many respects, there may be enough different circumstances to call for a different action on our part (such as the difference of dealing with a persistent errorist or a weak brother in outwardly similar circumstances). The applications suggested in this study should not be applied mechanically, but evangelically.

Basic applications of the principle: All expressions of fellowship are a unit

Joint use of the means of grace

All Lutherans agree that every joint use of the means of grace is an expression of fellowship. Christians are expressing fellowship whenever they encourage one another by worshiping together (Hebrews 10:24,25; Colossians 3:16). Sharing the Lord's Supper is obviously an expression of fellowship between the participants (1 Corinthians 10:17). Therefore, we are to worship and commune only with Christians with whom we are in doctrinal agreement. We cannot invite pastors who reject teachings of the Bible to preach in our churches, nor can our pastors preach in heterodox churches. This applies both to regular Sunday services and to special services of every sort. Christians should not attend Communion with congregations or individuals who adhere to false doctrine.

Financial support

Scripture clearly states that anyone providing financial support to a teacher of religion is expressing fellowship with him or her. This is true whether this teacher is one's own pastor or someone whose work is being done elsewhere. The Philippians were partners in Paul's work through the financial support that they sent to him (Philippians 1:5; 4:15). On the other hand, those who support or encourage false teachers are partners in their evil deeds (2 John 11). They are accomplices of an evil act, just as much as the individual who drives the getaway car for a bank robber or who hides a fleeing murderer. We, therefore, may not provide financial support or any other form of assistance to pastors, missionaries, or professors or to any form of church organization that persists in false teaching in spite of admonition.

Recognition of another's ministry

Fellowship is expressed by mutual consultations to resolve doctrinal questions and by agreeing to divide mission fields (Acts 15; Galatians 2:1-10). We, therefore, do not participate in religious studies and consultations with heterodox churches (except in efforts to eliminate the errors that separate them from us), nor do we agree to divide mission responsibilities with them.

Church fellowship is expressed by the exchange of fraternal greetings. Such greetings may be expressed by a handshake (Galatians 2:9); by a kiss (Romans 16:16); and by the exchange of fraternal greetings, which is so common in Paul's letters (Romans 16:1-16). Fellowship is also expressed by the "letters of recommendation" that are common in the New Testament (Romans 16:1-3; 2 Corinthians 8:16-23; 3 John 12).

Present-day practices that are parallel to these biblical customs are the handshake of recognition and welcome given at an ordination, a confirmation, or the acceptance of a new pastor into our synod; the exchange of greetings and commendations offered at church anniversaries or conventions; the granting of letters of transfer to another congregation; and the recommendation of pastors and teachers to other churches. We, therefore, do not transfer members to heterodox churches, nor do we convey congratulations and best wishes to the conventions of such church bodies. Our representatives may attend conventions or meetings of churches with whom we are not in fellowship (such as the LCMS) as observers, in order to obtain accurate, firsthand information about what is happening in those bodies, but they do not participate in worship, prayers, or discussions, nor do they deliver official greetings to such meetings. (Obviously there are many exchanges of greetings that are not an expression of church fellowship, such as a social greeting when meeting an acquaintance.)

Charity work

Today cooperation in Christian charity is sometimes regarded as mere "cooperation in externals," but it was not so regarded in the New Testament. The Macedonians urgently pleaded with Paul for the privilege of sharing in (that is, having fellowship in) the charitable service to the saints in Jerusalem (2 Corinthians 8:4). The goal of this charitable work was not merely to relieve human need, but to glorify God together. "This service that you perform is not only supplying the needs of God's people but is also overflowing in many expressions of thanks to God. Because of the service by which you have proved yourselves, men will praise God for the obedience that accompanies your confession of the gospel of Christ" (2 Corinthians 9:12,13). The spiritual motivation and the fellowship that are an essential part of Christian charitable work are emphasized throughout 2 Corinthians 8 and 9.

We, therefore, do not join with heterodox churches in charitable work nor in the operation of charitable institutions. When the Synodical Conference was dissolved, arrangements were made for an orderly dissolution of shared charitable work. (It is, of course, possible to do charitable work outside of the framework of religious fellowship, as is done in many secular charities.)

Prayer

Prayer is always an act of worship. We cannot say, "This prayer is simply an act of friendship or sociability." Prayer is always a religious act. All prayer, therefore, should be offered in accordance with the biblical principles of fellowship.

There are times when praying for a person is an expression of fellowship with him, for example, when praying for the success of an individual's ministry (Romans 15:30-32; 2 Corinthians 1:11) or in Jesus' high priestly prayer (John 17). There are, of course, many other circumstances when praying for a person is not an expression of fellowship, as when Christians pray for the enemies of the church or when we pray for the government (1 Timothy 2:1,2). Our prayer for false teachers should be that God will lead them back to the truth.

Praying in the presence of a person is not the same as praying with a person. Paul had no hesitance to pray in the presence of heathen on board the ship (Act 27:35), but he did not join their heathen prayers nor ask them to join in his. Simultaneous silent prayer within a group that is not united in doctrine is not an expression of prayer fellowship.

Praying *with* a person, however, is always an act of joint worship and therefore an act of fellowship. The disagreement between the Wisconsin and Missouri Synods concerning the doctrine of fellowship discussed in Part II of this book centered on the propriety of praying with people with whom we are not in doctrinal agreement, particularly with the leaders of heterodox Lutheran churches.

There is little specific treatment of the subject of prayer fellowship in the New Testament. As we saw earlier, prayer is simply treated as one expression of fellowship among many others. The early Christians "devoted themselves to the apostles' teaching and to the fellowship, to the breaking of bread and to prayer" (Acts 2:42). However, nothing in Scripture suggests that prayer should be treated any differently from any other expression of fellowship. Since God-pleasing prayer always flows from faith, every prayer is either an expression of faith (and therefore an act of worship), or it is an abomination. There is no middle ground. If true prayer is always an act of worship, joint prayer calls for the same unity of doctrine as any other act of worship. "Have nothing to do with them" and "keep away from them" cannot mean "pray with them." We, therefore, do not pray with Christians who are adherents of false doctrine.

12

Dealing with Special Problems
and Hard Cases
Part 1: Situations Dealing
with Our Own Services

Remember the purpose of the principles
of church fellowship

When we find ourselves struggling with a particularly difficult decision concerning the application of the principles of church fellowship, it is often helpful to remember the purpose of the principles of church fellowship. The principles are not ends in themselves. God gave them for the good of people's souls. When you are wrestling with a hard case, weigh each course of action available to you by honestly evaluating whether it will promote or work against one of the basic goals of the scriptural principles of fellowship:

1. Love leads us to warn the adherent of false teaching against his errors in the hope that he can be won to repentance (Matthew 18:15; 1 Timothy 1:3-5; 2 Timothy 2:25,26; Titus 3:10).

2. Love leads us to warn others against the errorist, so that they do not fall victim to his false teaching (1 Timothy 4:1-6; 2 Timothy 4:2-5; Titus 1:10-14). We have a special responsibility toward those weak in the faith (Jude 22,23).

3. We must avoid even the appearance of going along with error, even in matters that are adiaphora (Galatians 2:3). If a false teacher teaches falsely about an adiaphoron, we will not go along with him even though the matter in question is an adiaphoron.

4. We must separate from false teachers to protect ourselves from the dangerous poison of error, which is a threat to our souls (Galatians 5:9; 2 Timothy 2:17).

In hard cases we should ask ourselves, "How can I best give a clear testimony against error to the false teacher, to his adherents, and to everyone else who observes my action? How can I best win them for the truth?"

Some difficult areas

Closed Communion

WELS Pastors normally give Communion only to members of their congregations and visitors from WELS congregations and from synods in fellowship with WELS. Very rarely, unusual situations may arise that permit an exception to this regular practice. For example, a WELS member's mother who belongs to the Missouri Synod visits her daughter and suddenly becomes critically ill. She is hospitalized, and no LCMS pastor is available to minister to her. As she faces death, the WELS pastor who visits her in the hospital at her daughter's request could commune her since her immediate spiritual needs would be the paramount concern.

The private setting in which the action occurs lessens the likelihood of the offense that would be caused by such an action in a public worship service. Naturally, the normal requirements for being properly prepared to receive the Lord's Supper would apply. We could never, for example, commune someone who does not recognize the presence of Christ's body and blood, for he or she would be eating and drinking to his or her own judgment.

In asking whether it is possible to justify such exceptions to our normal practice, we may consider Jesus' evaluation of a similar "hard case," which permitted an exception to a ceremonial law God had given to Israel (Mark 2:27). The rule governing the situation was clear: non-priests were not allowed to eat the consecrated bread from the tabernacle (Leviticus 24:9). Yet Jesus did not condemn the priests or David for allowing David's men to eat the sacred bread in an emergency situation (1 Samuel 21:1-6). Furthermore, Jesus stated that even the law against work on the Sabbath permitted exceptions for the priests offering sacrifices or for anyone helping individuals or even animals in distress. The Pharisees' mistake was that they had forgotten that "the Sabbath was made for man, not man for the Sabbath" (Mark 2:27). We shouldn't forget that fellowship principles were made for man; man wasn't made for fellowship principles. If we remember that God desires "mercy, not sacrifice," we won't condemn the innocent (Matthew 12:7).

Some Lutheran writers of unquestioned orthodoxy say that the Lord's Supper is never enough of an emergency to allow for an exception to the rule, since the Lord's Supper is not an absolute need for salvation. But David's men would probably not have starved in one day, and the people who came to be healed on the Sabbath could have waited till Sunday. Jesus, nevertheless, does not condemn the exceptions that were made in order to help them.

We should, however, be very careful that exceptions do not undermine the principle or the normal practice, which still stands. Exceptions will normally occur only in cases in which we can establish that the person is properly prepared to receive the Lord's Supper but there is not time to fully explore the issues raised by the person's affiliation with a heterodox Lutheran church, or the person has lost the mental capacity to understand those issues.

Cases in which a person, for convenience' sake, wants to attend Communion both in a WELS congregation and in an ELCA or LCMS congregation, such as when Midwesterners spend the winter in the Sun Belt or when students are away at school, are not emergency situations. In such circumstances we owe the people a clear testimony that they cannot keep one foot in each camp. Since attendance at the Lord's Supper is not often an emergency need, exceptional cases will be very rare.

When members of another Lutheran synod that is not in fellowship with WELS are visiting services in a WELS church because they are disturbed by the liberalism in their church and they are considering becoming members of WELS for confessional reasons, we will encourage them to regard themselves as communicant members of their present church until they have given their testimony against the false teaching of that church, their testimony is not accepted, and they are, therefore, compelled to leave. If they are leaving their previous church for confessional reasons, they will understand and appreciate our careful stewardship of the Lord's Supper, and they will realize that they cannot be on both sides of the fence at the same time.

In determining cases of Communion fellowship, we must consider everything the Bible tells us about the Lord's Supper in 1 Corinthians 10 and 11. This is the *Lord's* Supper, not ours. His directions determine our practice. To attend the Lord's Supper in our churches, a person must: (1) believe in Christ so he can remember and proclaim his death, (2) recognize the presence of Christ's true body and blood so that he does not bring judgment upon himself by his eating and drinking, (3) be able to examine himself, and (4) be repentant for all his sins. In addition, he must be united with us in doctrine so we can truly be "one body" as we eat and drink together (1 Corinthians 10:17).

We call the Lord's Supper *Communion* because three communions or fellowships are involved: communion with God through faith; the communion of the body and blood of Christ with the elements of the bread and wine; and the communion of faith, that is, the fellowship between all of those who attend together. To participate in Communion in a God-pleasing way, an individual must understand and participate in all three of these communions. Those who participate without such understanding bring judgment rather than blessing upon themselves.

We do not allow our own children to attend the Lord's Supper until they have been carefully instructed and examined so that they may receive the Sacrament as a blessing. We ask our own members to announce for Communion and to prepare themselves to attend. We owe the same love and concern to those from outside. We exclude people who have not been instructed in our churches from attending Communion with us not in order to harm them, but to help and protect them.

To permit people to attend the Lord's Supper without proper knowledge and preparation is as irresponsible as it would be for a doctor to dump all of the medicine out on his waiting room table and to tell the patients to help themselves. A pastor, as a doctor of the soul, is as responsible for careful diagnosis and instruction of his patients as a doctor of the body is to his. If people attend the Lord's Supper at our churches without receiving instructions in our teachings, this would be as reckless as signing a contract they have never read or joining an organization without knowing what it stands for. Love requires us to exercise careful stewardship of the Lord's Supper.

Today we cannot assume that even those coming from other Lutheran churches have received thorough preparation for the Lord's Supper or sound instruction in the teachings of God's Word. For this reason also we cannot practice Communion that is open to all Lutherans. Love requires us to practice the Lord's Supper within the close circle of our own fellowship.

Because our practice of closed Communion can become a very emotional issue for those whom we ask not to attend the Lord's Supper and for our own members when we ask their friends or family not to attend, it is important that our congregations do everything they can to promote an understanding of the loving goals of our practice and to prevent misunderstanding and offense. Among the ways in which we can do this are the following:

1. We should provide ongoing instruction in the meaning of the Lord's Supper so that members understand why we treat it so carefully.

2. We should train the members of the congregation to inform visitors whom they bring with them about our Communion practices in advance so visitors are not surprised to find they cannot receive the Lord's Supper in our congregations.

3. We should make announcements in the bulletin and before Communion so that visitors understand the loving concerns that lie behind our practice. Such announcements must be carefully and clearly worded, since visitors may not understand such terms as "in fellowship with the teachings of this church" or "properly prepared to receive the Lord's Supper."

4. The pastor or trained greeters can be available before the service to provide a brief explanation to visitors. They may offer to explain our practice more fully later or may provide visitors with a tract that explains our practice.

What should the pastor do when someone he does not recognize appears at the altar? Should he commune the person or pass him by? If our Communion practice has been explained in advance as suggested above, the pastor need not accuse himself of irresponsible administration of the Sacrament if he distributes the elements to someone he does not recognize. In such cases the responsibility rests with the communicant. Visitors from sister congregations should announce to the pastor before the service to spare him from this dilemma. The pastor will make an effort to speak to any unknown communicant after the service to clarify the situation. If a person appears at the altar who the pastor knows has been warned not to attend, the pastor will not commune him.

In obedience to God's Word we stand in reverence and awe before the Sacrament of Christ's body and blood, given and shed for us. As congregations and pastors, we will want to administer and use this Sacrament as he directs so that the bonds of fellowship within our congregations will be strengthened. We will carefully warn everyone against improper reception of this sacrament and make every effort to reach out to others to win them to faith and repentance and to prepare them for a beneficial reception of the Lord's Supper.

Funerals

Our regular practice is that WELS pastors conduct a Christian funeral only for people who are members of our fellowship, since the funeral includes a recognition of the deceased's Christian confession and life. This means we normally bury only members of our own congregations. However, exceptional circumstances may arise.

It may happen that a WELS pastor was ministering to a nonmember during his or her last illness. In response to the pastor's presentation of the gospel, that individual confessed faith in Christ. After the person's death, the pastor learns the deceased had been a nominal member of the Masonic Lodge. Normally our churches would not conduct a Christian funeral for such a person, since the religious beliefs and practices of the Masonic Lodge contradict the Bible. But in this case, the deceased had not had a chance to "set his house in order." On the basis of the person's confession of faith, the pastor who had served him could conduct the funeral, but to avoid confusion or offense he would explain the circumstances to his church council and/or congregation, and he would not allow the Masons to have any role in the Christian funeral.

Sometimes military representatives or representatives of veterans groups will seek to address the mourners after the committal of a veteran. There is no problem with this if they simply present the family with a flag or offer a few words of appreciation for the veteran's service. But occasionally military chaplains will make remarks that are inappropriate and in some cases even unscriptural. The family and pastor should try to prevent this by respectfully informing the military representatives that the deceased's own pastor is conducting the funeral and that if they wish to speak, they should confine themselves to an expression of gratitude on behalf of the military. If such chaplains push themselves on the family by insisting on speaking after the service has ended, the responsibility for their remarks rests with them, not with the pastor or family.

Because the death of a loved one is a very emotional situation, it is important that pastors and congregations regularly remind their members of our funeral practices and of the reasons for them so that people do not first learn about them in the stressful situation of trying to arrange a funeral for a loved one. Pastors should also make every effort to evangelize the unchurched relatives of their members while they are still alive, when speaking the gospel to them can still do some good.

Participation in our services by nonmembers

If it is a violation of the scriptural principles of fellowship for us to participate in the services of heterodox churches, why do we allow members of heterodox churches or even unbelievers to be present during our services and to participate in the hymns and prayers?

It is wrong for us to participate in prayers, hymns, or creeds in any worship setting that supports error or grants equal rights to truth and error, such as the services of a heterodox church or an ecumenical service. Our services, however, are not such a compromised setting, since no rights or recognition are being given to error. Visitors of another faith who are present are not providing their own input to our services; they are receiving our doctrine. These are our services, not joint services. Visitors are not receiving the impression that there are no doctrinal differences that separate them from us. The fact that they cannot attend Communion in our churches gives them a clear testimony that they are not in fellowship with our congregations.

We admittedly do have a stricter practice concerning participation in the Lord's Supper than we do for joining in the hymns of the congregation. Part of the reason for this relates to fellowship concerns: coming forward to the Lord's Supper is a very visible confession of fellowship with the other communicants. This is one reason we treat the Lord's Supper with special care.

There is, however, an additional reason for closed Communion, that is, our responsibility to be sure that all communicants are properly instructed and prepared so that they do not partake of the Sacrament to their own harm, as discussed above. We cannot assume such preparation on the part of people who are not of our fellowship. We, therefore, must not allow them to attend the Lord's Supper, so that they do not bring judgment upon themselves by their attendance (1 Corinthians 11:29).

Even in the early church, nonmembers were not excluded from the common service, but only from the celebration of the Lord's Supper. Our general practice has been this: We do object to our members joining in the services of the heterodox because this gives the appearance of supporting false teaching; we do not have the same objection to prospects or visitors appearing to give assent to our services, which do not promote false doctrine.

If visitors do choose to participate in hymns or other elements of our services, their participation may imply an acceptance of what is being taught. So visitors of another faith who recognize this can, and often do, refrain from participating in the liturgy and hymns when they are present in our services to witness an event such as a baptism. The choice is theirs—to participate in worship that is offered on the basis of our confession or to refrain from participation since they are unsure of our position.

Other involvement in worship

The involvement of choir members, organists, choir directors, soloists, etc., in worship seems to fall into a category between receiving the Lord's Supper and singing hymns. Their involvment in worship does not require proper spiritual preparation in the same way as participating in the Lord's Supper does, but they are a more visible, public testimony of fellowship than sitting in the pew and joining in the hymns. We urge members to join the choir as a way of expressing their faith and serving the Lord. We want our church musicians to be committed ministers of music, who are able to make more than a mechanical contribution to the worship of the church. Church musicians are public representatives of the church, with a prominent public role. They, therefore, should be members of the congregation or its fellowship.

A secondary, practical consideration is the effect our practice may have on wavering or indecisive prospects. If we allow people who are not yet ready to make a commitment to membership to participate in the ministries of the congregation as if they were members, we may be encouraging them to continue their indecision. Withholding the privileges of membership will make it clear to them that they cannot continue to straddle the fence, but must make a decision. To permit them to make a commitment to serve the church before they are even committed to joining it is to put the cart before the horse. There might, however, be exceptional circumstances in which a committed person could be permitted to join the congregation or to serve it in special ways before completing all of the lessons of a membership class. Such cases would be dealt with on an individual basis.

In real life, however, disputes that arise concerning the musical participation of nonmembers in our services are rarely due to the presence of such sincere seekers, who are coming to the congregation to receive instruction in the truth. Problems are much more often due to one of two causes. First, someone has concluded that the congregation does not have adequate musicians among its members and must seek elsewhere for competent organists and directors. Such musicians may be hired with the rationale that they are just mechanics pushing the keys and collecting their pay. If all parties share this understanding of the job, perhaps it can be argued that this practice is no different than hiring a janitor, but is it really true that enhancing worship is as mechanical a function as sweeping the church floor? It is hard to understand how anyone could find much joy or satisfaction in such an arrangement. In such cases, it would be wise for the congregation to stop and ask itself, "Are we reaching outside our fellowship for musicians to fill our musical *needs* or our musical *wants*? Will our services be a better testimony to our faith if we gladly serve the Lord with the best talents he has given us or if we hire the best talents available, even if it means going outside our faith?" If the Lord has not given us anyone who can sing or direct, maybe it is not yet time for us to have a choir. (The rapid development of high-quality computerized music will soon diminish the perceived need to look to outside sources for musicianship.)

The second major source of conflict is the desire of members to have nonmembers participate in wedding services and the like. Here again we can ask the same questions as above: "Do we want this person to participate to meet musical *needs* or musical *wants*? Will the wedding service be a better testimony to our faith if we use the talents God has provided within our fellowship of faith or if we place our desire for musical beauty ahead of giving an unambiguous testimony to the truth?" If the reason for wanting nonmembers to participate in the service is not musical quality, but personal friendship, a second factor comes into play. Is there an unwillingness to give a clear and honest testimony to friends and relatives concerning the doctrinal differences that divide us? Is it really love for our friends to allow them to hold the impression that the doctrinal differences that divide us are not that important? If there are doctrinal differences separating us from those who desire to participate in the wedding, love requires that we give a clear testimony to them of the seriousness of the doctrinal differences that prevent them from taking a visible, active role in a service of the church.

We can help our members and their friends understand the reasons for our position if we give regular, clear instruction on the nature of a church wedding. What happens in a church wedding? The Word of God is proclaimed, we pray, we praise God, and people declare that they intend to obey God's will. A church wedding is, therefore, no different from any other worship service, except that God's Word and our worship are applied very directly to the marriage of two people.

Scripture teaches us that only people who agree with the teachings of the church should lead its services. Wouldn't it be strange if we invited someone who did not agree with our beliefs to speak a message from God's Word to us? Isn't it just as strange to invite such a person to sing a message from God's Word or to remind us of such a message by playing the melodies that bring it to our minds? For this reason, our practice is that we do not permit people from outside our fellowship to serve as organists and soloists during services of our churches.

The practice of allowing such participation in a wedding by nonmembers before the invocation or after the benediction, which a few congregations apparently have adopted, is not to be recommended because it too easily becomes a way of evading the issue. Is it valid to claim that the music immediately before and after the service is not part of the worship? If the music has been well-chosen, the organist has begun our worship of God even before any members of the wedding party have entered the church. The second problem is that such a practice can easily give the impression that we are more concerned to uphold the letter of an arbitrary law than we are to fulfill the evangelical purpose of our fellowship practice, which is to give a clear testimony against false teaching. Is it really love for friends and family to let them think that the doctrinal differences that divide us are not that harmful and that practicing the biblical principles of church fellowship is a burden we seek to evade?

When pastors give careful, loving, and ongoing instruction about the biblical principles of church fellowship, it is less likely that these problems will have to be dealt with at emotional occasions such as weddings and funerals, when there is great pressure to compromise to avoid conflict. It must be granted, however, that our principles and practices of fellowship will remain offensive to many people, just as many other parts of God's Word are.

Children's services and school choirs

Many of our congregations do not exclude children of nonmembers from singing in church on such occasions as a service following the completion of vacation Bible school. Can we justify this discrepancy from our practice concerning church musicians that we have just discussed? It is normally clear to everyone that the children are simply presenting what they have been taught in class. They are not independent preachers, who adhere to a message different from that of the congregation. They are learners receiving instruction from the congregation. If a situation arose in which Baptist parents said, "We think it's great that our children can come to your vacation Bible school each summer and sing in your service even though we disagree with your doctrine of Baptism," we would not let their children participate, since we would have to give a clear testimony against their error.

The aim of the principles of church fellowship is not to prevent people from hearing, accepting, and proclaiming the truth. It is to give a clear testimony against false teaching. If we remember that, we will generally have a good idea of the action we should take in a given case.

Similar questions arise about the activities of nonmember students in our elementary schools, high schools, and colleges. Should these students participate in chapel services, choral presentations, and the like? Here the root of the problem often lies partly in unclarity concerning the enrollment policy. Are the nonmembers in our schools evangelism prospects, that is, willing learners whom we are instructing with the hope of winning them for our fellowship? If so, they can participate in the school's activities in the same ways in which visitors participate in congregational worship, as discussed earlier.

If, on the other hand, these students and their parents are Christians who hold doctrinal convictions that are not in agreement with our position, who intend to maintain their present fellowship, but who are willing to pay for the services of our school for the perceived educational benefits, we should not treat them as if they were in fellowship with us, for then we are sending confusing, mixed signals. We should also honestly examine our reasons for permitting their enrollment in our school under such circumstances. Are we trying to win them away from their heterodox churches? Are we providing them with educational services for a fee as a way to increase the income of our school? If we are simply providing them with educational services for a fee, we might do well to ask ourselves if this is a valid function of our Christian schools.

In short, we should treat nonmember students in the same way that we treat other visitors to a congregation. If they are mission prospects being instructed in the truth, they can participate in the regular instructional program and worship, but they should not take a leading role in worship or serve as public representatives of the school, as, for example, touring choirs do. Since our main concern in the practice of church fellowship is clear public testimony to the truth, there is some difference between in-house chapel services on the one hand and public concerts or tours to congregations on the other, but even in-house events should give a clear testimony to all students and parents, members and nonmembers alike.

The same general practice would be applicable to elementary schools, high schools, and colleges. Our seminary is in a different situation because it exists for the sole purpose of preparing pastors for churches of our confessional fellowship. In very exceptional cases a student who was coming to us for confessional reasons might be admitted before he had joined a WELS congregation. But he could not represent the seminary or the church in public, even in such roles as practice teaching, until he had taken a clear confessional position by means of his church membership. In such cases of transfer to our seminary for confessional reasons, it is normal that the questions of the student's membership and confessional stand are resolved before enrollment. We do not accept students from outside our fellowship who are looking for a general theological training.

Baptismal sponsors and witnesses

Baptismal sponsors, that is, those who promise to help raise a child in the true teachings of the Bible, must be members of our fellowship. Those who merely witness that the baptism was performed need not be of our fellowship. If sponsors are being used, we should instruct prospective parents of the value and importance of choosing sponsors who qualify to be a positive Christian influence on the child, especially if the parents die. The new baptismal order in *Christian Worship,* which emphasizes the responsibility of the congregation and parents and de-emphasizes the role of sponsors and witnesses, will probably reduce problems with this issue.

No confessional role is involved in being witnesses to a wedding, so the principles of fellowship do not come into play in choosing members of a wedding party.

Receiving funds from outside the church

The church sometimes receives funds from outside its membership. These may be offerings given by visitors, or they may be gifts or grants offered by foundations, corporations, or the government. In some cases the gifts are offered spontaneously by the giver. In other cases the church might seek these grants or make formal application for gifts that have been offered. How does the reception of such gifts relate to the principles of church fellowship?

First, concerning gifts from individuals: We need not reject offerings made by visitors, but we should be very careful that nonmembers are not receiving a faulty impression concerning the motivation for Christian giving. If there is a self-righteous motive for the gift, we must warn the person against such giving and may have to reject the gift to make the point clearly. For example, if an excommunicated person offered a large gift to the congregation, that had disciplined him, in order to express his attitude "I am not good enough for you, but I bet my money is," the congregation should reject the gift to make it clear "what [we] want is not your possessions but you" (2 Corinthians 12:14). If it is not clear what the nonmembers' motivations for such gifts are, the solution is simple—ask them. We cannot let desire to receive a gift stand in the way of a clear testimony to the giver.

If foundations or corporations are involved, the situation often becomes murkier. There is the least problem when corporations simply offer to match charitable contributions of their employees or customers, who assume personal responsibility for where the gift goes and for how it is used. For example, an investment in a mutual fund may carry with it the offer to match, up to a certain limit, a gift the investor makes to a church college. These matching gifts are an extra return on the investment, an incentive to hold that investment. Neither the investor nor the school have any religious fellowship with the company.

But what if the corporation takes upon itself the responsibility to determine where the grants go? They then must certainly accept a measure of responsibility for how those funds are used. Further problems arise if the group promotes itself as a religious association that is joining in the work of the church. Are the gifts advertised as a spiritual service offered by the corporation and its members? These practices would raise valid concerns about the propriety of receiving funds from such corporations or foundations.

Most of the concern and controversy about this issue in WELS has involved grants received from two Lutheran fraternal insurance companies, Aid Association for Lutherans (AAL) and Lutheran Brotherhood.

There was little problem before 1961, when AAL served only members of the Synodical Conference and Lutheran Brotherhood served members of other Lutheran churches. After the dissolution of the Synodical Conference, however, AAL decided to serve Lutherans from all Lutheran bodies. This raised problems since AAL bylaws implied fellowship between its members. In 1973, as a result of this unclarity, the WELS Conference of Presidents declared a moratorium on applying for grants from AAL. Subsequently, AAL changed its bylaws to remove the implications of fellowship. The moratorium was then lifted. In 1979 the WELS convention accepted a lengthy report on this issue.[38] The report concluded that receiving grants from such corporations does not in itself imply fellowship with the corporations nor with the other organizations that receive grants from them. However, the report also warned that vigilance is necessary lest such grants undermine Christian stewardship or give the impression of unity and fellowship where they do not, in fact, exist. The report also expressed concern that company advertising or publicity sometimes gave the impression of fellowship, contrary to the explicit statements of the bylaws.

The 1979 report also concluded that Lutheran Brotherhood's statement of purpose implied a spiritual fellowship between its members and that WELS, therefore, should not seek grants from Lutheran Brotherhood. The Lutheran Brotherhood statements were later changed, and WELS institutions have received grants from them since then. In both cases WELS went on record as being ready to give up gifts that carried with them an implication of fellowship where none existed.

Conclusion

In all of these situations our chief concern is "How can we give the clearest testimony to the truth, both to the weak and to the strong, to the errorists and to the adherents of the truth?"

13

Dealing with Special Problems
and Hard Cases
Part 2: Working with Others

Attending services of heterodox churches

We should worship only with those with whom we are in agreement in doctrine. A person may be present at services of heterodox churches for reasons other than worship, for example, to attend the wedding or funeral of a relative or friend or to observe the worship of that church body in order to obtain correct information about it. But in such cases the observer should not participate in the worship, rites, or prayers of the heterodox group.

1 Corinthians 8:10 ("If anyone with a weak conscience sees you . . . eating in an idol's temple, won't he be

emboldened to eat what has been sacrificed to idols?")
may simply be a rhetorical question referring to something
that should never happen, but it may refer to a real situation in which a Christian was invited by friends or family
to attend a festive meal in one of the rooms at a heathen
temple that served a function similar to our rented ban-
quet halls. There would not necessarily be anything wrong
with such attendance, as long as it did not lead weak
Christians to sin against their consciences by eating meat
sacrificed to idols. But 1 Corinthians 10:14-21 states very
specifically that Christians are not to participate in any
meals that are rites honoring an idol.

On his return to his homeland after he had been
healed of his leprosy by Elisha, Naaman's duties as an official of the Syrian government required him to enter heathen temples in the company of the king. When the
king, who was leaning on Naaman's arm, bowed to the
idol, Naaman had to bow too, but his bowing was not
worship of the idol Rimmon. Elisha told him, "Go in
peace." Naaman made a clear confession of his new faith
by sacrificing only to the Lord on soil he had brought
with him from Israel (2 Kings 5:15-19).

When we find ourselves in circumstances similar to
Naaman's, we should do whatever is necessary to give a
clear testimony. We should not join in the prayers of heterodox churches. We normally would not fold our hands
or bow our heads as if praying. We would not kneel or
cross ourselves during prayers to Mary or the saints. There
might be other circumstances in which one could stand
during the prayers without giving a confusing signal to the
worshipers. It would depend in part on whether the visitor
and his or her purpose for being there were known to the

worshipers. A person would do whatever would convey the message of polite nonparticipation.

Attending schools with a religious affiliation

Sometimes WELS members may wish to attend schools that have some sort of religious affiliation. Does this involve them in religious fellowship with the churches that sponsor the schools?

Sometimes the school may be a university or college—like Marquette, St. Olaf's, or one of the Concordias—that has a religious affiliation but accepts all students into its academic programs on a "pay-for-services" basis. Many WELS members attend such colleges. We may not be happy with these choices in cases in which the students could attend one of our WELS colleges, but there is not necessarily any fellowship involved. Attendance at chapel services and participation in worship would, however, involve fellowship and should be avoided. Taking a religion class would not necessarily involve fellowship, but could be a danger to a person's faith, just as many classes in a secular university might be.

Sometimes in areas where there are no WELS schools and the public schools are undesirable, WELS parents may wish to have their children attend a Christian high school or elementary school. They sometimes feel that they are faced with a choice between two evils, a public school that promotes unchristian values or a religious school that may entangle them in unscriptural fellowship. This is admittedly a very difficult situation. It may well be that neither option is God-pleasing. Maybe home schooling, a prep school, or even moving are options.

But let us suppose that the only viable options are public school or religious school. What then? We must distinguish between situations that may confront us with temp-tation or danger to our faith and situations that require us to sin. God may well require us to face temptation and defeat it. He does not require us to sin. Let us look at the two options in this light.

No public school forces students to believe in human-ism, evolution, and anti-Christian morality (safe sex, abor-tion), but the required curriculum may force them to be exposed to teachers and materials that advocate such views. Being exposed to such views may be a danger, but it is not in itself a sin. It may, in fact, be an opportunity to testify against such views. The students and their parents do not have to accept or practice these views. They should oppose their inclusion in the school curriculum and seek to be excused from exposure to them.

In a non-Lutheran religious school, the children may also be endangered by exposure to unbiblical teaching. Such subtle false doctrine may be more dangerous to faith than the more crass and obvious errors present in some public schools. Usually children attending a private reli-gious school have waived any right to oppose or con-tradict the teachings of that school. If the school, as a condition of attendance, requires children to participate in worship that violates the biblical principles of fellow-ship, this does not merely expose the children to danger. It also requires them to sin. This a parent cannot accept or allow.

Limited to the choices described above, I would use the public school, but would carefully seek accurate informa-tion about what was being taught, speak against those classes that present unscriptural material, seek relief from them where possible, and teach my children the truth that opposes those teachings.

Difficult situations such as this are sometimes a matter of judgment. Two sets of Christian parents in very similar environments may come to different conclusions. In such situations we should be cautious about judging the decisions made by others. Doubtful cases are not a place to exercise church discipline. When confronted with such a dilemma ourselves, we should become fully informed, discuss our situation with a few trusted Christian friends, and make the best decision we can, trusting the Lord's promise "[God] will not let you be tempted beyond what you can bear. . . . He will also provide a way out so that you can stand up under it" (1 Corinthians 10:13).

Working for religious institutions

Our members are sometimes employed by churches, religious schools, or institutions affiliated with a church. Many of these jobs, such as janitorial or secretarial work and food service jobs, usually involve no religious fellowship. Our churches and schools sometimes employ nonmembers in such positions. Civil rights laws requiring nondiscrimination in hiring may also come into play in some of these cases.

Other jobs, such as teaching or musical leadership, may involve a worker in the religious ministry of the church or may require participation in worship. Accepting such a job would then involve a compromise of fellowship principles.

Other cases may be unclear, such as some teaching or coaching positions. In such cases a person should examine each situation on its own merits or demerits. How does the employer define the job? What are the requirements of the job? We cannot necessarily assume that the requirements of the position are the same as they would be for a similar position in our churches.

Ambiguous situations are sometimes a matter of judgment. Two Christians in very similar circumstances may come to different conclusions. As stated earlier, in such situations we should be cautious about judging the decisions made by others. Doubtful cases are not a wise place to exercise church discipline.

Public testimony and conferences
with heterodox churches

We should always be ready to give clear testimony to the truth whenever we have the opportunity, even to groups and individuals who oppose the truth. Paul was ready to testify and to defend the truth even in heathen temples and hostile synagogues, but he never compromised the truth to gain a hearing, and he withdrew from those who rejected his testimony.

Examples of situations in which we might have the same opportunity to witness to the truth are (1) "free conferences" with individual Lutherans who have a genuine interest in becoming informed about doctrinal differences between their synods and ours; (2) doctrinal discussions, outside the framework of fellowship, with church bodies not in fellowship with us; or (3) presentations of our beliefs to a non-Christian group.

In a free conference, individuals who believe that they may be agreed in doctrine or that they may be able to reach agreement in doctrine meet to discuss those doctrines that appear to be points of difference separating their respective church bodies. They do not represent their church bodies. Our goal in attending such meetings with confessional Lutherans from other synods with whom we are not in fellowship is to encourage individuals in those synods to make a clear confession of the doctrines of

Scripture to their own church bodies and to separate from those church bodies if their testimony is not accepted.

The ultimate aim of free conferences is to help confessional Lutherans in heterodox fellowships find like-minded Christians so that they will separate themselves from those unionistic fellowships and seek the fellowship of an orthodox church. Such free conferences may begin with silent prayer, which acknowledges that each participant is a Christian sincerely seeking the truth, but that unity in that truth has not been reached yet.

WELS is always ready to meet with representatives of churches with whom we are not in fellowship, such as the LCMS or the CLC, anytime they desire to discuss the differences that separate us, as long as such meetings are progressing toward reaching a scriptural resolution of the dispute and are not seeking a compromise between truth and error. Such discussions should begin with a study of the Scripture passages dealing with the doctrines that have been the cause of the division and should lead to one joint doctrinal statement clearly resolving the past difference on the basis of Scripture. The WELS Commission on Inter-Church Relations would not participate in meetings that were merely being used to give an impression of cooperation and agreement between the church bodies and were not making a concerted effort to remove doctrinal differences.

I once was invited to present the topic "Who is Jesus?" to a large group of Muslims with a Muslim debater opposing my view. No one on either side of the divide had the impression that either I or the Muslim speaker was watering down his position or seeking a compromise between the two positions. As a result of this debate, members of the local mosque invited me to come and discuss Christianity and Islam with them. I continued to do so until the leadership of the mosque threw me out for raising interest in Christ there. We should not hesitate to make use of such opportunities to testify to the truth, as Paul did in Acts 19:8-10.

We obviously would not participate in joint worship or prayers in any of the situations described in the preceding paragraphs.

Since our twofold goal is giving testimony to the truth and avoiding any support for error, our general principle is that we are willing to give a clear testimony to a heterodox church or a heathen religion "on their turf" anytime we have the opportunity to do so, but we refrain from giving heterodox or heathen teachers an opportunity to make propaganda for their teachings among Christian people. Sometimes the situation is not clear-cut, and one must weigh the benefits of the opportunity to witness against the possibility of causing confusion or offense. There is a certain amount of danger of offense in any situation in which you are offered an opportunity to "take turns" with heterodox teachers or unbelievers, but at times one may be able to make a clear confession even in such circumstances.

When I was a home-mission pastor, each week the local newspaper in our small town ran a short sermon written by one of the local pastors. For convenience, the schedule for these sermons was set up by the local ministerial association. One day the editor of the paper called me in and said that she knew that because of my principles of fellowship (with which she did not agree) I did not participate in the local ministerial association, but she felt that the community should be exposed to my views, and that she, therefore, wanted to set up a schedule for me to provide sermons for the paper. She offered to do this directly with me so that I could write for the paper without going through the ministerial association. Our church was notorious enough in town for its "intolerance and narrow-mindedness" that I didn't have much concern that anyone would think I was joining with the other members of the local ministerial association, so I accepted the offer.

I was once invited by a district pastors conference of the LCMS to appear on a program with representatives of the LCMS and ELCA in which we would present our respective views about the critical issues confronting American Lutheranism. Certainly this situation provided both the opportunity to testify and the possibility of misunderstanding and offense. I would have been happy if this "opportunity" had never come my way since such situations can be very tense, but I did not refuse the invitation outright. I wrote back to the program committee and told them that if I came, I could not participate in worship or prayer, and I provided them with an outline of what I would have to say about the doctrinal issues that separate the LCMS from ELCA, and WELS from ELCA and the LCMS. I offered them the opportunity to "uninvite" me. They said they wanted me to come anyway, so I attended and made my presentation. I received the impression that it was a worthwhile effort that gave encouragement to the confessional pastors who were present.

If you as a pastor or layperson find yourself confronted with such ambiguous opportunities, carefully weigh the situation using these questions: (1) What can I do to give a clear presentation of the truth to those who need to hear it? (2) How can I avoid the impression of compromise with error? Then seek the advice of some wise fellow Christians. If you feel that you are in over your head, do not hesitate to ask fellow Christians to help you or even to take your place in giving testimony to the group. Prayerfully decide on your course of action. Explain the reason for your action to your congregation and other fellow Christians if this will help prevent misunderstanding and offense. Give your testimony. Leave the results up to God. Don't agonize too much over whether you can prevent anyone from taking offense and criticizing you. Jesus was not deterred by the fact that both his friends and foes often disapproved of the places and people he chose to receive his testimony to the truth (Luke 7:34,35; John 4:27).

If you find yourself suspecting that brothers or sisters made the wrong decision in such a hard case, talk to them about it, and give them the benefit of the doubt. If you feel that they were clearly in the wrong, you have an obligation to demonstrate this on the basis of Scripture, not your own feelings.

When we are presented with an opportunity to give a clear testimony and to win people for the truth, we should give a greater priority to the opportunity to win those in error than to the possibility that someone somewhere might take offense that we spoke there. For those who are caught in error, the opportunity to hear and heed our testimony might be a matter of spiritual life or death. We must exert every possible effort to bring even one lost sheep back to the fold.

In situations that do not provide the opportunity to testify against error, such as meetings that are designed to promote sharing and exchange of information about "externals" between church bodies that are not in fellowship, I would be more concerned about avoiding offense and even the appearance of accommodation with error. I would try to be careful not to leave the other participants with the impression that the doctrinal differences that divide us are not such a big deal after all. Such opportunities, however, should not be rejected out of hand since they may provide the chance for a more substantial presentation of the truth at least to some individuals.

Family and friends

The principles that govern our practice of fellowship with individuals are no different from the principles that govern our public relationships with groups of Christians. We are to warn all who are holding false doctrine against that false doctrine. If they cling to that doctrine in spite of our admonition, we must not practice fellowship with them. It makes no difference if they are family or friends. We cannot place family ties and friendship ahead of our loyalty to God and his truth (Matthew 10:32-39; 12:46-49).

The one practical difference between the two situations, however, is that when religious fellowship with family or friends involves only private actions that will not give public offense, we may consider not only the public confession they make through their church membership, but also their private, personal confession.

It is the public confession of their church that governs our public fellowship relationships with our family or friends. If they are members of a heterodox church, we must base our public relationship with them on the public confession and practice of their church. In other words, we should not participate in the services of that church with them, although there may be occasions when we attend services there, as discussed earlier. As a testimony of love we must warn them against the false teachings of their church by refusing to participate in its worship.

In our private relationships with them, we may also consider their personal confession. For example, if they are dissenting members of a heterodox Lutheran church, who object to its false teaching and are fighting against it, we may recognize them as one in faith with us in our private relationships with them. We will encourage them to battle for the truth, but we will also warn them that they must leave that false church if their admonition is rejected. The private confession of faith they make to us and the public confession they are making by their church membership are in contradiction, and they must take steps to bring them into harmony.

If they are unaware of the unscriptural beliefs or practices of their church and, thus, are not knowingly adherents of false doctrine, we will urge them to become accurately informed about the teachings and activities of their church, which they are supporting by their offerings. Here too they should take steps to remove the compromise from their confession.

If their private confession, however, reveals that they are aware of the false teaching of their church and defend it, we should not practice religious fellowship with them even in our private relationships. We must warn them strongly that their adherence to false doctrine is a barrier preventing fellowship between us and them, and, more importantly, their adherence to false doctrine threatens their relationship with God.

How should we put these principles into practice? First, let us consider our actions in our own home. There is no reason for a Christian family to abandon prayer and family devotions when others are present with them at the table. This is no different than having guests with us at church. The host may proceed with prayer or a devotion as normal. We have no more reluctance to have our prayers heard by others than Paul did on his voyage to Rome

(Acts 27:35). Our prayer may be a good testimony and example to them. We may, however, feel that we should not force our guests to be a "captive audience" to prayers or devotions that they do not approve of, but this is a question of manners and tact, not an issue of fellowship. We must consider whether this is a good opportunity to expose them to the Word or whether imposing our worship on them without their consent will create resentment and a backlash against hearing the Word.

When we are guests at the table of a person who is not of our faith, and he speaks his prayer in our presence, we will permit him to do so without disturbing him, even if we cannot join him in his prayer. We should not, however, join together in the prayers of adherents of false doctrine, either by asking them to lead our family in prayer or by joining together with their prayer.

The same principles would apply to a member of a WELS church in a religiously mixed marriage. If one spouse is a non-Christian, the Christian partner may pray for and in the presence of the non-Christian husband or wife. Obviously, they cannot pray together. If the other spouse is a member of a heterodox church and ridicules or rejects the beliefs of our member, joint prayer is hardly possible. If the other spouse's membership in a heterodox church is seen as a matter of weakness in understanding, joint prayer may be possible in the privacy of the home. The Christian partner in a mixed marriage will try to win the other by a good example of piety and patience (1 Peter 3:1-7). Situations in mixed marriages may vary greatly, and Christian spouses will be concerned not to do anything that is spiritually harmful to their partner. Much love, tact, and truthfulness is needed in such a situation.

We should also mention that a lack of unity in religion is not a valid scriptural reason for divorce. "If any brother has a wife who is not a believer and she is willing to live with him, he must not divorce her. And if a woman has a husband who is not a believer and he is willing to live with her, she must not divorce him (1 Corinthians 7:12,13).

Civic religious ceremonies

Scripture teaches that people should not join together in worship and prayer unless they agree in doctrine. We therefore should not participate in any religious activity that gives equal status to truth and error.

At civic religious ceremonies in the United States, such as opening prayers at sessions of government or other civic events, all denominations and even non-Christian religions are given equal status, as when the duty of leading the service or providing an opening prayer is rotated among various clergypersons. Such a practice is very confusing to those who are weak in their understanding. Such a practice gives the impression that all religions are more or less interchangeable and equally pleasing to God.

I was once asked to conduct a baccalaureate service for the local public high school together with the liberal Lutheran pastor, who had driven some of the members of his congregation into my congregation by his false teaching. What impression would it have given to the members of both congregations and to people in the community if we would have conducted such a service together? It would have appeared that the dispute that led my members to leave his congregation was nothing but a personality conflict, rather than an act of confession compelled by a difference in doctrine. In the minds of many it would have confirmed the all-too-common view that it really does not matter what you believe, since all religions are basically the same and can cooperate.

Such a false impression can easily be given even when the adherents of opposing views do not participate in the same service, but take turns in successive services. Love requires us to give a clear testimony against religious indifference which treats truth and falsehood as equals.

Pastors of many denominations do not believe that agreement in doctrine is necessary for joint prayer and worship, so they see no problem in worshiping with people who hold unscriptural views. Others may feel that they can participate in such arrangements as a testimony to their own view, without giving the impression that they are granting equal recognition to error, but such a distinction will seldom be clear to the general public. Our pastors, therefore, should not participate in such civic services and devotions.

Just as a person may occasionally be present at services of a heterodox church for reasons other than to join in the worship, a member of our church may be present on civic occasions that are opened with unionistic prayers. For example, a member of Congress might be present when legislative sessions begin with prayer. He or she, however, should not join in such prayers or assist in setting them up, but should use his or her influence to eliminate prayers that are intended to unite people of various faiths in worship without agreement in doctrine.

This problem will be most common in countries that have a state religion. Naaman appears to have been thinking of such a civic occasion when he asked Elisha to pardon his presence at heathen prayers (2 Kings 5:17-19). As an aide to the king of Syria, his civic responsibilities often required him to be present for heathen rites, to rise and kneel when everyone else did, but he would not join in that worship. Elisha does not condemn him for his request.

Participation in political action groups and social groups that have a religious perspective

Can WELS members belong to political action groups that are formed to preserve, protect, and promote traditional "Judeo-Christian values" through education, legal defense, lobbying, and related activities, and that represent the concerns of men and women who believe in these values? Such groups are organized to fund and implement political action that is aimed at influencing government policy on such issues as taxation, abortion, education, and homosexuals in the military.

Christians, of course, should not belong to any organization that requires them to accept principles or teachings that are contrary to the Bible. Nor should they join in prayer and worship with groups or individuals who hold teachings contrary to the Bible. They should not offer financial support to them. The Masonic Lodge and Shriners would be examples of such organizations.

The task of drawing clear lines may become more difficult when the organization in question is not a religious organization and has no religious requirements, but it does have some religious activities or motivations attached to it. In such cases a number of considerations may help Christians decide to what degree, if any, they may be involved.

For the sake of obtaining information, Christians can buy books or subscribe to periodicals even from groups whose philosophy they reject and which they would not join. For example, our synodical libraries subscribe to many periodicals that are published by groups our students and professors could not join. The subscription price is a payment for goods received.

A similar situation may exist with groups such as the YMCA. This organization has a Christian mission, and full membership involves religious activity. But the organization recognizes a different level of "membership" at which the participants simply become users of the athletic facilities in exchange for a certain payment. Such payment for the use of the facilities would not involve a person in the religious fellowship of the group.

As citizens, WELS members may participate in political action groups that try to influence legislation and government policies in order to promote moral standards that will protect their neighbors' property and lives. For example, members of WELS Lutherans for Life might also be members of a nonreligious right-to-life group in which they join with people of other faiths or of no faith at all in efforts to influence government policy concerning abortion and euthanasia. In the WELS' own right-to-life organization, changing people's hearts through God's law and gospel should be the primary goal and method. In the secular group changing people's minds through education and changing their conduct through civil law would be the goals.

A problem arises when such organizations begin to blur the line between religious groups and nonsectarian political action groups by introducing prayer or other religious activities into their program. (The same problem can arise in groups as different as the local garden club, an ethnic society, or a business organization.) If such activities are an essential activity of the group and are prominent in its program, members of our churches should not join the group or participate in its activities. If the objectionable activity is incidental to the purpose and program of the group (such as prayer at the opening of the meeting of the garden club), Christians should refrain from participating in that activity and should express their objections to the practice, but they may participate in the regular, secular functions of the group.

An additional problem with many political action groups that are under heavy Reformed or Catholic influence is that they often confuse the responsibility of the church and its members (that is, changing people's conduct by first changing their hearts with the gospel) with the responsibility of the state and its citizens (that is, changing people's conduct by enforcing beneficial laws). Many of these groups believe that efforts to change society by lobbying and legislation are a direct part of the mission of the church.

Christians should be clear on the distinction between what they do as church members (for example, preaching the Sixth Commandment to lead people to repentance) and what they do as citizens (for example, seeking laws against various forms of sexual immorality as a protection to individuals and society). If you are a member of a group that seems to be confusing the roles of church and state, try to get the group refocused on the proper goals. If the confusion is deeply embedded in the group's program and philosophy, discontinue your membership in the group.

A third problem arises when such groups see themselves as an ecumenical leaven for bringing diverse churches together without agreement in doctrine, as in the statement of a pro-life leader, "The Lord is using unborn babies to unify his Church."[39] If this is an aim of the group, we should not participate, even if its activities are otherwise commendable. This is often a factor in the growing cooperation between Catholic and Evangelical social action groups.

In all of these situations, we should distinguish practices and attitudes that are inherent in the group's philosophy and program from occasional aberrations that are the views or actions only of isolated individuals.

In short, don't join any organization without inquiring about its beliefs and practices. If either its beliefs or practices conflict with the Bible, don't join unless the group is willing to remove the offensive practices. If incidental violations of biblical principles arise, object to them and do not participate in them. If, subsequent to joining, you find that membership is involving you in beliefs or practices contrary to Scripture or if activities involved in membership trouble your conscience, quit.

Political action by church groups

As stated above, it is not the duty of the church to lobby the government for laws that enforce Christian conduct. The church may petition the government when laws are being considered that would interfere with the mission of the church, such as laws that would take away the religious freedom of Christian schools. In such cases, representatives of our schools have joined in lobbying efforts with other groups who share our concerns in the area, such as the LCMS and the Catholic Church. Such activities do not involve joint prayer and worship, but defense of civil rights.

Outside speakers at our events

Various WELS organizations or schools may invite lecturers from outside our fellowship to present information to their group. This does not involve fellowship if no worship or religious instruction are involved, but only the giving of information. In situations that might create unclarity, such as a series of public lectures presented at a seminary or college of our fellowship, it is wise to make a specific announcement that these lectures are being presented outside the framework of fellowship. This is regularly done at the Bethany Reformation Lectures. If you think that the lecturer might have a misconception of his or her role, speak to the person in advance.

The same principles apply to academic associations, such as church history or archaeology societies.

Publications

We have not regarded every instance of publication, sales, or advertising of an author's materials as an expression of fellowship with him or her. Northwestern Publishing House has sold and published numerous works of non-WELS authors, and it has given another publishing house rights to reprint and distribute The People's Bible commentary series. Both of these actions are intended to promote the widest possible distribution of sound Lutheran material.

On the other hand, cooperative efforts to develop religious materials require unity in doctrine. If doctrinal agreement does not exist between the authors and editors who are working on a project, certain parts of the books may be incompatible with the convictions of some of the participants. Even when each author is made responsible for his own material, the impression of fellowship with false teaching can readily be given. For this reason, our seminary faculty recently declined an invitation from outside our fellowship to participate in a project to develop a series of Bible commentaries for pastors.

In the case of The People's Bible series, we are taking advantage of an opportunity to have our materials reach a larger audience, which will benefit from their scriptural presentation. In the case of the Bible commentary series for pastors, we were concerned not to have our names attached to a project in which doctrinal positions might be presented that are not in agreement with Scripture on such issues as church fellowship, church and ministry, and the Antichrist. Neither case necessarily involves fellowship, but the effect and the likely impression is different in the two cases.

WELS scholars have provided input and evaluations during the process of preparing new Bible translations, such as the New International Version, since the goal of such projects is to provide an unbiased translation for all Christians, which will not be slanted toward doctrinal interpretations of particular denominations. In such projects, we do not participate in worship or prayer with translators with whom we are not in fellowship.

If we sell materials that contain doctrinal errors, we should provide warnings about their content for those who may not be equipped to detect the errors.

14

Conclusion

In 1 Timothy 1, immediately after telling Timothy to oppose false teachers, Paul says, "The goal of this command is love, which comes from a pure heart and a good conscience and a sincere faith" (verse 5). We dare not lose sight of the reason that we practice the biblical principles of church fellowship: The goal of this command is love—love for the errorists, love for their victims, love for anyone who is threatened by false teachings, and love for God and his truth.

To withhold the truth from someone who needs it, to silently go along with error—this can never be love. To be silent in the presence of error, which sweeps people away to hell, makes us as guilty—no, more guilty—as the person who silently stands by and watches a fire burn up a house and its sleeping inhabitants. Love requires me to cry out; love requires me to warn. To be silent because I don't want to offend anyone, because I don't want to be labeled intolerant, because I love the praise of men more than the praise of God—this is not love; this is selfishness. Let us never be guilty of sleeping on duty like unfaithful watchmen. We must sound a clear warning against all false teaching. *We must work together for the truth. We can do nothing against the truth.* These two principles direct us in all the decisions we must make concerning the practice of church fellowship.

We must, of course, always be on guard against pride and a self-righteous attitude. We must guard against tactlessness and against inconsistencies that will cause people to lose confidence in our judgment. Even as we speak strongly against the errors of false teachers, we will deal patiently with their victims as we try to gain them for the truth (Jude 12,22). But we must not let a recognition of our own imperfection intimidate us into a neglect of our God-given duty to warn against error. Acceptance of our duty to warn against error must always be paralleled by a willingness to listen to warnings and admonition when we need them. If we first pull the plank out of our own eye, we will see clearly to pluck the speck of sawdust out of our brother's eye (Matthew 7:5).

If we keep our eyes focused on the blessed purposes for the principles of church fellowship—to testify to the truth and to warn against error—we will not dread the task of applying these principles to all areas of our lives as Christians. We will recognize that this is just one more way we can serve our neighbors in love as we work together for the truth.

The principles of church fellowship are not a handicap but a blessing. WELS right now is enjoying the benefits of the scriptural principles that our past and present leaders have fought for. We are reaping the harvest of doctrinal unity that they planted and cultivated. Although we will always face doctrinal problems as long as the world continues, we enjoy as a gift from the Lord a degree of peace, harmony, and unity of purpose that is not found elsewhere in the large bodies of American Lutheranism.

We too seldom stop to marvel at this blessing and to kneel and thank God for it. We are provided with a steady stream of sound Christian literature like The People's Bible. When we call a pastor, we can have a very high degree of confidence that he will teach the same sound doctrine as the pastor who departed. When we or our children move to another area of the country, we can feel optimistic that the WELS congregations there have the same doctrinal position as the congregation we are leaving. The biblical principles of church fellowship that we have studied are one of the main tools the Lord has used to provide us with such blessings.

If we want to continue to enjoy such blessings, we must continue to practice church discipline in a loving, evangelical way. When doctrinal disagreement arises in our midst (as it surely will), we must study the issue in Scripture, identify and warn against false teaching, and separate from anyone who clings to it. Only in this way can the unity we enjoy be preserved.

God has given us rich blessings through the principles of church fellowship. This doctrine is not an embarrassment. It is the way God establishes and preserves this blessed fellowship we share. We pray that God may always keep us faithful in the practice of this doctrine, so that we may hold on to the treasures of the gospel which he has entrusted to us.

Appendix
WELS Statement on Church Fellowship
(1970)

Preamble

Church fellowship is a term that has been used to designate both a *status* and an *activity*. Both usages lie very close together, and one flows out of the other. The two usages follow the general dogmatic distinction of *in actu primo et actu secundo*.

Church fellowship can be *defined* as the *status* in which individuals or groups, on the basis of a common confession of faith, have mutually recognized one another as Christian brethren and now consider it God-pleasing to express, manifest, and demonstrate their common faith jointly.

Church fellowship can also be *defined* as the *activity* which includes every joint expression, manifestation, and demonstration of the common faith in which Christians (individuals or groups), on the basis of their confession, find themselves to be united with one another. (Mutual recognition of one another as Christian brethren is itself one such "joint expression" of common faith in which Christians on the basis of their confession find themselves to be united with one another.)

For very practical reasons, we have preferred to treat church fellowship in our Theses as a term designating an *activity* since the inter-synodical tensions have to do more with church fellowship as an activity than as a status. Both as a status and as an activity, church fellowship needs to be distinguished from the spiritual fellowship of faith in the holy Christian church (*Una Sancta*) which it is meant to reflect but with which it cannot simply be identified. For in the case of hypocrites, who have not yet been revealed, church fellowship is still called for, though the fellowship in the holy Christian church (*Una Sancta* fellowship) is actually not existing. On the other hand, people may in God's sight be united in the fellowship in the holy Christian church (*Una Sancta* fellowship) and yet not have warrant to practice church fellowship here on earth.

We also felt that our definition of church fellowship was general enough to include both proper and improper practice of church fellowship, for the definition itself does not specify what constitutes an adequate confession on the basis of which individuals or groups may properly find themselves united in a common faith. For is there not in all church fellowship the assumption present that an adequate confession exists? Our presentation under the points of B sets forth what constitutes a proper confession, the marks of the church (*notae purae*), on the basis of which Christians may properly find themselves united in a common faith.

The Theses

Church fellowship is every joint expression, manifestation, and demonstration of the common faith in which Christians on the basis of their confession find themselves to be united with one another.

A. How Scripture leads us to this concept of church fellowship.

1. Through faith in Christ, the Holy Spirit unites us with our God and Savior. Galatians 3:26; 4:6; 1 John 3:1.

2. This Spirit-wrought faith at the same time unites us in an intimate bond with all other believers. 1 John 1:3; Ephesians 4:4-6; John 17:20,21. Compare also the many striking metaphors emphasizing the unity of the church, e.g., the body of Christ, the temple of God.

3. Faith as spiritual life invariably expresses itself in activity which is spiritual in nature, yet outwardly manifest, e.g., in the use of the means of grace, in prayer, in praise and worship, in appreciative use of the "gifts" of the Lord to the church, in Christian testimony, in furthering the cause of the gospel, and in deeds of Christian love. John 8:47; Galatians 4:6; Ephesians 4:11-14; Acts 4:20; 2 Corinthians 4:13; 1 Peter 2:9; Galatians 2:9; 5:6.

4. It is God the Holy Ghost who leads us to express and manifest in activity the faith which he works and sustains in our hearts through the gospel. Galatians 4:6; John 15:26,27; John 7:38,39; Acts 1:8; Ephesians 2:10.

5. Through the bond of faith in which he unites us with all Christians, the Holy Spirit also leads us to express and manifest our faith jointly with fellow Christians according to opportunity: as

smaller and larger groups, Acts 1:14,15; 2:41-47; Galatians 2:9; as congregations with other congregations, Acts 15; 1 Thessalonians 4:9,10; 2 Corinthians 8:1,2,18,19; 2 Corinthians 9:2.

(Before God every activity of our faith is at the same time fellowship activity in the communion of saints. 1 Corinthians 12; Ephesians 4:1-16; Romans 12:1-8; 2 Timothy 2:19.)

6. We may classify these joint expressions of faith in various ways according to the particular realm of activity in which they occur, e.g., pulpit fellowship; altar fellowship; prayer fellowship; fellowship in worship; fellowship in church work, in missions, in Christian education, and in Christian charity. Yet insofar as they are joint expressions of faith, they are all essentially one and the same thing and are all properly covered by a common designation, namely, church fellowship. Church fellowship should therefore be treated as a unit concept, covering every joint expression, manifestation, and demonstration of a common faith. Hence, Scripture can give the general admonition "avoid them" when church fellowship is to cease (Ro 16:17). Hence, Scripture sees an expression of church fellowship also in giving the right hand of fellowship (Gal 2:9) and in greeting one another with the fraternal kiss (Ro 16:16); on the other hand, it points out that a withholding of church fellowship may also be indicated by not extending a fraternal welcome to errorists and by not bidding them Godspeed (2 Jn 10,11; cf. 3 Jn 5-8).

B. What principles Scripture teaches for the exercise of such church fellowship.

1. In selecting specific individuals or groups for a joint expression of faith, we can do this only on the basis of their confession. It would be presumptuous on our part to attempt to recognize Christians on the basis of the personal faith in their hearts. 2 Timothy 2:19; Romans 10:10; 1 John 4:1-3; 1 Samuel 16:7.

2. A Christian confession of faith is in principle always a confession to the entire Word of God. The denial, adulteration, or suppression of any word of God does not stem from faith but from unbelief. John 8:31; Matthew 5:19; 1 Peter 4:11; Jeremiah 23:28,31; Deuteronomy 4:2; Revelation 22:18,19. We recognize and acknowledge as Christian brethren those who profess faith in Christ as their Savior and with this profession embrace and accept his entire Word. Compare Walther's "Theses on Open Questions," Thesis 7: "No man has the privilege, and to no man may the privilege be granted, to believe and to teach otherwise than God has revealed in his Word, no matter whether it pertains to primary or secondary fundamental articles of faith, to fundamental or nonfundamental doctrines, to matters of faith or of practice, to historical items or other matters subject to the light of reason, to important or seemingly unimportant matters."

3. Actually, however, the faith of Christians and its manifestations are marked by many imperfec-

tions, either in the grasp and understanding of
Scriptural truths, or in the matter of turning
these truths to full account in their lives. We are
all weak in one way or another. Philippians 3:12;
Ephesians 4:14; Ephesians 3:16-18; 1 Thessalonians 5:14; Hebrews 5:12; 1 Peter 2:2. Compare
Walther's Thesis 5: "The church militant must
indeed aim at and strive for absolute unity of
faith and doctrine, but it never will attain a
higher degree of unity than a fundamental one."
(Cf. Thesis 10.)

4. Weakness of faith is in itself not a reason for terminating church fellowship, but rather an
inducement for practicing it vigorously to help
one another in overcoming our individual weaknesses. In precept and example, Scripture
abounds with exhortations to pay our full debt of
love toward the weak.

   a. General exhortations. Galatians 6:1-3; Ephesians 4:1-16; Matthew 18:15-17.

   b. Weakness in laying hold of God's promises in a
   firm trust. Matthew 6:25-34.

   c. Weakness with reference to adiaphora in
   enjoying fully the liberty wherewith Christ has
   made us free. Romans 14; 1 Corinthians 8 and
   9. The public confession of any church must
   on the basis of Scripture establish, however,
   which things are adiaphora, so that it may be
   evident who are the weak and who are the
   strong. Romans 14:17-23; 1 Corinthians 6:12;
   10:23,24.

d. Weakness in understanding God's truth, and involvement in error. Acts 1:6; Galatians (Judaizing error); Colossians (Jewish-Gnostic error); 1 Corinthians 15; 1 Thessalonians 4:10-12,14; 2 Thessalonians 3:6,14,15; Acts 15:5,6,22,25. Note how in all these cases, Paul patiently built up the weak faith of these Christians with the gospel to give them strength to overcome the error that had affected them. Compare Walther's Theses 2, 3, 4, and 8.

5. Persistent adherence to false doctrine and practice calls for termination of church fellowship.

   a. We cannot continue to recognize and treat anyone as a Christian brother who in spite of all brotherly admonition impenitently clings to a sin. His and our own spiritual welfare calls for termination of church fellowship (excommunication). Matthew 18:17; 1 Corinthians 5:1-6.

   b. We can no longer recognize and treat as Christian brethren those who in spite of patient admonition persistently adhere to an error in doctrine or practice, demand recognition for their error, and make propaganda for it. Galatians 1:8,9; 5:9; Matthew 7:15-19; 16:6; 2 Timothy 2:17-19; 2 John 9-11; Romans 16:17,18. If the error does not overthrow the foundation of saving faith, the termination of fellowship is not to be construed as an excommunication. Moreover, an excommunication can only apply to an individual, not to a congregation or larger church group. The "avoid them" of Romans 16:17,18 excludes any contact that would be an acknowledgment and manifestation of church fellowship; it calls for a cessation of every further joint expression of faith. (Cf. 1 Corinthians 5:9-11. Compare Walther's Theses 9 and 10.)

c. Those who practice church fellowship with persistent errorists are partakers of their evil deeds. 2 John 11.

From all of this, we see that in the matter of the outward expression of Christian fellowship, the exercise of church fellowship, particularly two Christian principles need to direct us, the great debt of love which the Lord would have us pay to the weak brother, and his clear injunction (also flowing out of love) to avoid those who adhere to false doctrine and practice and all who make themselves partakers of their evil deeds. Conscientious recognition of both principles will lead to an evangelical practice also in facing many difficult situations that confront us, situations which properly lie in the field of casuistry.

On the basis of the foregoing, we find it to be an untenable position

A. To distinguish between joint prayer which is acknowledged to be an expression of church fellowship and an occasional joint prayer which purports to be something short of church fellowship;

B. To designate certain nonfundamental doctrines as not being divisive of church fellowship in their very nature;

C. To envision fellowship relations (in a congregation, in a church body, in a church federation, in a church agency, in a cooperative church activity) like so many steps of a ladder, each requiring a gradually increasing or decreasing measure of unity in doctrine and practice.

*Full attention needs to be given in this statement to the limiting terms: "insofar" and "joint." The "insofar" is to point out that it is indeed only in their function as joint expressions of faith that the use of the means of grace and such other things mentioned as Christian prayer, Christian education, and Christian charity all lie on the same plane. In other respects the means of grace and their use are indeed unique. Only through the means of grace, the gospel in Word and Sacrament, does the Holy Spirit awaken, nourish, and sustain faith. Again, only the right use of Word and Sacrament are the true marks of the church, the marks by which the Lord points us to those with whom he would have us express our faith jointly.

For anything to be a "joint" expression of faith presupposes that those involved are really expressing their faith *together*. This distinguishes a joint expression of faith from individual expressions of faith which happen to be made at the same time and at the same place. Certain things like the celebration of the Lord's Supper, the proclamation of the gospel, and also prayer, are by their very nature expressions of faith and are an abomination in God's sight when not intended to be that. When done together, they are therefore invariably joint expressions of faith. Other things like giving a greeting, a kiss, a handshake, and extending hospitality or physical help to others are in themselves not of necessity expressions of Christian faith. Hence, doing these things together with others does not necessarily make them joint expressions of faith, even though a Christian will for his own person also thereby be expressing his faith (cf. 1 Co 10:31). These things done together with others become joint expressions of faith only when those involved intend them to be that, understand them in this way, and want them to be understood thus, as in the case of the apostolic collection for the poor Christians at Jerusalem, the fraternal kiss of the apostolic church, and our handshake at ordination and confirmation.

Endnotes

[1]Augsburg Confession, Article VII:2, *The Book of Concord: The Confessions of the Evangelical Lutheran Church*, translated and edited by Theodore G. Tappert (Philadelphia: Fortress Press, 1959), p. 32.

[2]Formula of Concord, Epitome, Article X: 7, Tappert, p. 493.

[3]Werner Elert, *Eucharist and Church Fellowship in the First Four Centuries* (St. Louis: Concordia Publishing House, 1966).

[4]Martin Luther, *Luther's Works*, edited by Jaroslav Pelikan, American Edition (St. Louis: Concordia Publishing House, 1964), Vol. 27, p. 38.

[5]*Luther's Works*, Vol. 27, p. 41.

[6]Martin Luther, *What Luther Says: An Anthology*, compiled by Ewald M. Plass, 3 vols. (St. Louis: Concordia Publishing House, 1959), p. 812.

[7]Friedrich Balduin, *Tract on Cases of Conscience*, II, 6,7.

[8]Quoted in Adolf Hoenecke, *Ev. Luth. Dogmatik*, Vol. 3 (Milwaukee: Northwestern Publishing House, 1909), p. 441.

[9]The relevance of the actions at Thorn to 20th century disputes about prayer fellowship was considered both in the WELS pamphlet "Fellowship Then and Now" (pp. 29,30) and in the LCMS' "Theology of Fellowship" (pp. 18,19,22). The LCMS presentation minimizes the significance of the Lutherans' refusal to have joint prayers with the Catholics and Reformed, but it was the Missouri Synod's *Der Lutheraner* that first used the example of Thorn to justify the Synodi-

cal Conference's refusal to hold joint prayers with the Ohio and Iowa Synods early in the 20th century (Vol. 64, No. 7, 1908, p. 111). Accounts of this incident are given in Herzog's *Realenzyclopedie*, 1862 edition, Vol. 16, p. 105, and in the 1907 edition, Vol. 19, pp. 747,748.

[10]Thesis 7 of Walther's "Theses on Open Questions." Quoted in "WELS Statement on Church Fellowship." See page 167 in this book.

[11]See the tract "Fellowship Then and Now," which can be found in *Essays on Church Fellowship*, edited by Curtis A. Jahn (Milwaukee: Northwestern Publishing House, 1996), pp. 349-378.

[12]Bente delivered his essay in 1904 and had it published in *Lehre und Wehre*, 1905, pp. 97-115. An English translation of the essay may be found in the Wisconsin Lutheran Seminary Library Essay File, No. 124.

[13]Richard C. Wolf, *Documents of Lutheran Unity in America* (Philadelphia: Fortress Press, 1966), p. 401.

[14]Wolf, p. 399.

[15]Wolf, pp. 402,403.

[16]Both quotes are from Wolf, p. 406.

[17]Wolf, pp. 428,429.

[18]"A Statement," reproduced in *Concordia Historical Institute Quarterly*, Vol. 43, No. 4 (November, 1970), pp. 150-152. It can also be found in *Moving Frontiers*, edited by Carl S. Meyer (St. Louis: Concordia Publishing House, 1964), pp. 422,423.

[19]Theodore Graebner, *Prayer Fellowship* (St. Louis: Concordia Publishing House, 1946).

[20]Wolf, pp. 424-426.

[21]See the WELS pamphlet "Entrenched Unionistic Practices," authorized by the Commission on Doctrinal Matters, Wisconsin Ev. Lutheran Synod, 1961.

[22]See "Theology of Fellowship," *Synodical Conference Proceedings*, 1960, p. 45.

[23]"Unity in the Context of Theological Pluralism," cited in *Forum Letter*, Vol. 1, No. 8 (1972), p. 5.

[24]"Statement on Communion Practices," *Lutheran Standard*, October 16, 1979, p. 40.

[25]"Justification By Faith," *Origins*, Vol. 13, No. 17 (October 6, 1983), pp. 277-304.

[26]"The Nature and Implications of the Concept of Fellowship," Commission on Theology and Church Relations, The Lutheran Church—Missouri Synod, 1981, p. 43.

[27]*Lutheran Witness*, October, 1982, p. 34.

[28]*Lutheran Witness*, May 2, 1983, p. 4.

[29]Quoted in *Wisconsin Lutheran Quarterly*, Fall, 1988, p. 267.

[30]*WELS Proceedings*, 1957, p. 144. *Proceedings of the Northern Wisconsin District*, 1956, p. 61.

[31]*WELS Book of Reports and Memorials* (BORAM), 1993, p. 236.

[32]BORAM, pp. 236,237.

[33]BORAM, p. 240.

[34]For the full resolution, see *CLC Proceedings*, 1994, pp. 66,67.

[35]John Lau, "We Recommit Ourselves to Hold Fast to Sound Doctrine," *Journal of Theology*, 1994, p. 32.

[36]Michael Wilke, "What's Going On among the 'Conservative' Lutherans—Part II," West Central Pastoral Conference, Good Shepherd Lutheran Church, September 20-22, 1994, p. 3.

[37]Readers who want more information and the complete text of the joint statement should read the *WELS Book of Reports and Memorials*, 1993, pp. 232-241 and the CLC *Journal of Theology*, 1994, pp. 31-34.

[38]*WELS Proceedings*, 1979, pp. 49-65.

[39]*Focus on the Family—Citizen*, June 18, 1990, p. 2.

For Further Reading

Brug, John, Edward Fredrich, and Armin Schuetze. *WELS and Other Lutherans*. Milwaukee: Northwestern Publishing House, 1995.

Fredrich, Edward C. *The Wisconsin Synod Lutherans*. Milwaukee: Northwestern Publishing House, 1992, especially pp. 37-61, 198-208, the history of our relations with the LCMS and the CLC.

Jahn, Curtis A., editor. *Essays on Church Fellowship*. Milwaukee: Northwestern Publishing House, 1996. A reprint of important exegetical and doctrinal essays, pertaining especially to the debate between WELS and the LCMS. Includes "Fellowship Then and Now," mentioned in this book.

Lawrenz, Carl. "The Scriptural Principles Concerning Church Fellowship," in *Our Great Heritage*, Vol. 3. Milwaukee: Northwestern Publishing House, 1991.

Wolf, Richard C. *Documents of Lutheran Unity In America*. Philadelphia: Fortress Press, 1966. This book contains most of the original documents concerning inter-Lutheran relationships in America before 1966.

Scripture Index

2:18—34
2:19—15,166,167
2:24-26—54
2:25,26—118
3:1-9—30
3:13-17—30
4:2-5—118
4:3,4—30
4:14—29

Titus
1:10-14—118
3:9—34
3:10—30,49,55,118

Hebrews
5:12—168
10:24,25—17,45,111

James
2:1-5—37

1 Peter
1:22—52
2:2—168
2:4,5,9—14
2:9—165
3:1-7—149
4:11—39,167
4:12-16—109

2 Peter
2:1-3,13-20—34

1 John
1:2,3—58
1:3—19,165
1:7—14

2:19—26
3:1—165
3:16—28
3:17-19—52
4:1-3—167
4:1,5,6—27
4:3—36
4:6—25
5:2—28

2 John
9-11—26,169
10—24
10,11—46,166
11—112,170

3 John
4-8—53
5-8—166
5,6,8,12—24
8—24,25,58
9,10—26
12—47,112

Jude
3-10—34
12,22—160
18,19,22,23—54
22,23—118

Revelation
2:2,3—27
2:14-16,20,21—27
2,3—34
22:18,19—34,167
22:19—39

Subject Index

Organists 127,130

Persistent errorists 54-56,84
Political action groups 152-
154
Prussian Union 69

Rallies 82,83
Reformed 65,69,79,154

School
Attendance 139,140
Enrollment 131-133
Scouts 7,75
Shriners 152
Soloists 127,130
"Statement" of the 44

73,74
Synodical Conference 61,69-
71,76,78,84,85,89,90,99-
101,114,135

"Theology of Fellowship"
(LCMS) 76
Transfers 113

Weak brothers 54
Weddings 129,130,133
Worship services 131,132,
137-139

YMCA 153